LOOK BEYOND
Your
HORIZON

And You Will Be a High Achiever
in the Making

HO NEE YONG

PARTRIDGE
A Penguin Random House Company

To order additional copies of this book, contact
Toll Free 800 101 2657 (Singapore)
Toll Free 1 800 81 7340 (Malaysia)
orders.singapore@partridgepublishing.com

www.partridgepublishing.com/singapore

Contents

Preface

A man was toiling in the field under the scorching sun when a panic-stricken hare broke from cover and crashed headlong into a tree stump, with a fatal result. He was overjoyed that though he did not put in any effort, he was rewarded with a hare. From that day onward, the man sat by the stump, waiting for more hares to come and dash themselves against it. However, the second hare never appeared, while the field remained a wasteland. The moral of this story is that you should not put your trust to chance and windfalls.

You are responsible for your own life. A swift horse does not come from the backyard, and a warm chamber does not produce a pine that reaches the sky. When you strive hard to look beyond your horizon, you can be the swift horse and the gigantic pine. You can either be a roc, a legendary bird that can fly thousands of miles freely in the air, or a finch, a small bird which only hops up and down within a radius of a few dozen metres. You can either look at the world in its perspective from the sky or you can just live in solitude and be ill-informed.

The beginning is always the most difficult because it is farthest from the light at the end. Take your first initiative in reading through this book and be familiar with the nub of the satirical remarks of "The Thick Face and the Black Heart" in chapter 1, and learn about the two persons whom you must know very well in chapter 2.

When you take a broad and long-term view in life in chapter 3, you are going beyond the limit of your ideas, knowledge, or experience. Chapter 4's SMART Goals will give you an insight into the domains in goal setting, and the 36 stratagems in chapters 5 and 6 are to caution you of the hypocrisy and reality in life. Fly the extra mile in chapter 7, and you will be a high achiever in the making.

Ho Nee Yong
October 2013

Chapter One

The Twelve Genuine Words and the Two Brilliant Methods

The Study of the Thick Face and the Black Heart

I have chosen to begin this book by introducing you to Li Zongwu (1880-1943), who wrote a very popular cynical book, *Houheixue* (*The Study of the Thick Face and the Black Heart*), in 1912, depicting the historical Chinese heroes as having thick skins and black hearts. Lin Yutang (1895-1976), a Harvard scholar and an authority on China and Chinese culture, commented that scholars who had read Chinese and foreign books widely but had yet to read this book of Li were to regard this lost opportunity as a matter for regret. (Liu Si 2005a)

However, there are people who may not subscribe to Lin's statement and consider the reading of this book as an anticlimax to achieving a harmonious society. Nevertheless, there are also

1

others who feel that the book actually mirrors the basic instinct of human beings who veneer their "thick face and black heart" with a thin layer of integrity. In a society where morals gradually demand a higher premium, it is imperative that young people should equip themselves with the knowledge of *The Study of the Thick Face and the Black Heart* so that they will not fall into the bottomless pit of being shameless and evil in heart. Indeed, to say that there is relevancy of the book's biting sarcasm on many social ills in ancient China to our modern society is an understatement.

There were readers who complained to Li that his book was too difficult to comprehend for simple-minded people like them. They requested him to simplify his thought to benefit them. Li then asked one of them, "What would you like to do?" He replied, "I want to be a government official, and I want to have it on a grand and spectacular scale so that I can be recognised as a great statesman." Li then passed on to him the "six genuine words in begging for an official post," "six genuine words meant for serving officials," and "two brilliant methods in handling affairs." (Liu Si 2005: 16-22)

The Six Genuine Words in Begging for a Position as an Official

When a person seeks for a position as an official, he has to keep these words in mind:

Free (空)

The first genuine word means to be idle in two aspects. Firstly a person who begs for a post must be focused; he should not be working, trading, reading, or farming the land. Secondly he must have ample free time so that he will be patient and not be in a hurry. He must be able to wait for days and even years.

This word "free" is applicable when you graduate and apply for a job. You may send letters to as many companies as you can. You have to stop all your activities and concentrate on your job applications. You wait at home for the postman or emails to come every day. You have all the time in the world to look through the advertisement columns in newspapers or on the Internet for more job opportunities. Whether you are aspiring to be a government official or are looking for an executive position, be it senior or junior, in the private sector, you still have to stick to the word "free."

Drilling (or Working Hard) (贡)

This word is taken from the local dialect of Sichuan Province in China to mean working hard. Li's idea is that you must keep on drilling to get what you want. What is implied is that while you work on the old contact lists, you must also try your best to establish new networks. You should enlarge the old bases and drill for the new ones.

In real life, what you normally do after sending in your application forms for a job will be to work hard to contact your friends, both new and old. In a society where the culture of "looking for people for help" is prevalent, as distinct from the practice of meritocracy in First World countries, you may need to run up and down before you land yourself on the first job.

Boasting (冲)

This is blowing your own trumpet. The art of boasting and flattering can be divided into two parts: verbally and written. The verbal aspect can again be applied in two different situations, namely common places and in front of superiors; while the writing part can be in mass media like newspapers and magazines, as well as in the form of public display and the Internet.

In the economic market, where your diplomas and degrees may not be the only criteria in getting you a job, you are expected to market yourself during interviews. You tend to be at a disadvantage if you are too shy to discuss your abilities, which can be the deciding factor in your interviews. When this word "boasting" is applied, you not only tell the facts but also blow your own trumpet as loud as possible.

Flattering (捧)

When you flatter someone, you praise them excessively or insincerely to gain some advantage. You then become an outwardly kind but inwardly cruel person. Ill-bred people who use flattering words and phrases show themselves to be lacking in self-confidence, ability, and intellect. So if you want to command respect from others, you need to be genuine and sincere in your expressions. This is one of the twelve genuine words of Li for those who want to apply to be a government officer. As a human weakness is that we like to be flattered and that beggars have no choice, those who ask have to resort to flattery to get what they want. This calls for those who flatter to have a "thick face" and to say things which are against their conscience.

Threatening (恐)

Li considered this word to be important if you want to secure the post as an official. In ancient China, those in authority could hire and fire their subordinates as and when they deemed fit. However, they could also be threatened when their secrets or weaknesses gave others a handle to go against them. Nevertheless, you may use this tactic in subtlety to get what you want from the one who has the power to decide your future.

The Chinese proverb "hesitating to pelt a rat for fear of smashing the dishes beside it" or "spare the rat to save the dishes" shows us that when you apply the word "threaten" at the right time, you may get what you want from the one in authority. The latter has to hold back from taking action against you for fear of involving other people.

Giving (送)

There are two different types of presents to be given: big and small. For a high position, you need to give a big stack of money, while for a lower position, you might deliver hampers to the house or take the benefactor out to a meal. In modern economic terms, you are investing now when you give and reaping your returns later when you have secured your position as an officer.

Look around and you will be swarmed by the magnitude and power of giving. Although there are measures to stop the practice of giving to prevent government servants from accepting gifts during festival seasons, the givers can always make sure the gifts find their ways to the hands of the receivers. However, the fight against covert corruption may not have any actual effect if there is no self-discipline among the givers and the takers. Li mentioned this word as vital in The *Study of the Thick Face and the Black Heart,* because during his time in China in the early 1900s, when the country was both poor and weak, giving was the passport to getting things done.

The Efficacy of the Six Genuine Words

According to Li, when all the six words in begging for an official post have been meticulously personified, the almighty department head concerned would have to ponder and consider seriously the following salient points:

This man has come to me for help to be an official for a long time (first word: he has ample free time to spare); he and I are related in a way (second word: he works hard coming in and out of my office); he has some ability and wisdom (third word: the boasting of the man works well); he is good to me (fourth word: flattering); however, this man has evil ideas, and if I do not give him something, it may spell trouble for me (fifth word: threaten); at this point the powerful VIP looks back at the piles of glittering silver on his desk (sixth word: the effect of giving money and presents), and then he hangs out the card saying this post goes to So-and-So. (Liu Si 2005b: 17-18)

When the man has ultimately secured an official position, he is required to implement the essence of the next six genuine words, which Li had so generously showered on his followers.

The Six Genuine Words Meant for Serving Officials

Empty(空)

The word "empty" here refers first to circulars and approval letters which are devoid of contents. The subtlety of the written documents is worded in such a way that they mean nothing, or they are ambiguous. Secondly in handling affairs in the office, the official will take an equivocal attitude. His answer can be either positive or negative depending on the situation at the time of decision making. While carrying out policies resolutely, he has also secretly prepared a way for retreat when things go wrong. He will never get himself entangled in any controversy or scandal. This is a common practice among officials in countries with poor governance, resulting in low productivity and high corruption. Li's observation on the weakness of man in position could not have been more accurate indeed.

Servile (恭)

This means to be slavish or overly anxious to please someone. The official has an ingratiating and servile attitude towards his immediate superior. He also tries his very best to develop a relationship with the relatives, friends, and servants of his boss. He wags his tail to please the extended family of his master to gain favours from his boss. He has no stand on any policy, and the view of his master is his view, even if it does not make sense. However, you may also notice that in real life, the servile attitude accorded to the superior disappears the moment he is out of power. His courtyard that has been thronged with visitors will now have visitors who are few and far between. You can even catch sparrows on the doorstep of his house. Giving is therefore only given to someone who is in power and not one who is a lame duck.

Looking Displeased (绷)

This is the same as pulling a long face, and it has the opposite meaning of servile. This can be expressed in your smart attire to show that you are an important person, or it can be manifested in your speech and deportment. You are to act snobbishly. You can be flexible in applying "looking displeased" to anyone you think has no control over you. When you were in primary school, you might have seen teachers or headmasters put on an act when they wanted to discipline their pupils; they meant good and wanted to instill discipline among the pupils. The "looking displeased" as mentioned by Li is more of an insinuation that you cover your hypocrisy for an intended purpose and a selfish gain.

Fierce (凶)

According to Li, as long as your aim can be achieved, it does not matter whether the other person has to sell his children or wife. I should say that this is extremely vicious, and the executor has a face which is too thick and a heart which is too black; there is no humanity in him. The Chinese believe that of all the fiercenesses, the fiercest is that of poverty. When a person is a poor wretch, his temper is at its worst, which can easily trigger him off to rob or to kill. However, those officers who are not poor, comparatively, may only want more wealth to be added to their account. In the context of *The Study of the Thick Face and the Black Heart*, Li contended that officers who are greedy should show no mercy at all to anyone to get what they want. This explains why the Chinese people in the olden days were afraid to go to the government departments, for fear of being reprimanded by corrupt officials. Li, however, cautioned officials to temper the word "fierce" with humanity and morality to show that they cared for the people.

Deaf (聋)

When officials are deaf, they turn a deaf ear to their critics' derision. It does not matter to them that their poor performance is greeted with derisive comments because they pretend not to have heard them. Li reminded us that the "deaf" here is inclusive of blindness, which signifies that they are blind to written sarcastic criticism. Li implies that a corrupt official who stuffs his ears and refuses to listen will only hear and see when a stack of "white silver" is shown to him. He is then no more deaf and dumb. Throughout the history of China, the downfall of almost all dynasties was due to the emperors and their ministers who were deaf to the voices of the people. The analogy therefore is that when you are one of the deaf officials, you stand up to be counted as one of those who will be disgraced.

Amassing (弄)

This refers to amassing ill-gotten wealth for your own self. When you are already an official, this is the most appropriate time for you to do so. Before you secure the position as an official, you have already given the bribes and presents as investments. It is your turn now to reward yourself with the lucrative returns and swap your position from that of a giver to a taker. The eleven words before this are the means to an end to this twelfth word, "amassing." It is the time for you to be handsomely rewarded, albeit the crooked way. Li commented that if you are able to amass a fortune for yourself, even though it is too big a sum, do not be modest but just take and keep the money. Li did not elaborate on the twelve genuine words but expected those who would desire to be government officials to further study the topic and do research on their own. (Liu Si, 2005c: 20)

The twelve genuine words of Li represent his condemnation of corrupted administration and government officials during the turmoil of his time in the early 1900s in China.

The Two Brilliant Methods

Li was generous and insinuated enough to offer government officials two brilliant methods in handling office work on top of the twelve genuine words. It was an extra bonus to them.

The Method of Sawing the Arrow (锯箭法)

According to Li, when a person was shot by an arrow, the physician would saw off the shaft, leaving the arrowhead in the body before asking for his fee to be paid. On the question of why the arrowhead was not taken out, the physician said that it was the duty of a surgeon. The analogy is that serving officials who apply this method will just pen a few words like "It is illegal to do so and the officer concerned must take action to rectify it." "It is illegal" is sawing the arrow, and "the officer concerned" is the surgeon who is supposed to take action and solve the problem.

When you are approached by your friends for help, you can then say, "I totally agree with you on this matter. However, I need to discuss this with So-and-So." "I totally agree" is sawing the arrow; "So-and-So" becomes the "surgeon" who needs to solve the problem. When you saw the arrow, you stay clear of all the blames and hassles. Li commented that serving officials could do the sawing without asking their clients to seek the help of the surgeon to remove the arrowhead, or they simply would not saw the arrow but refer their clients straight to the surgeon for the removal of the whole arrow. (Liu Si 2005: 21) Indeed, this is the musical chair-type of dealing with the public when the grievances of the public are passed round in a vicious cycle by inefficient officials. The documents will go missing in the process, and that completes the round of sawing the arrow.

There is an old Chinese saying, "The *yamen* gate is open wide; with right but no money, don't go inside," which pictured the inefficiency and the corruption prevalent in *yamen*, the government departments in feudal China. The majority of the serving government officials then applied the method of sawing the arrow. The common people could only get things done when they bribed the officials with white silver, because the givers were forced to believe that with money you can even ask the ghost to do the grinding work for you.

The Chinese character for government officials is written as 官 (pronounced as *guan*) and it has two mouths or 口. Since the ancient time, the Chinese have always tried to avoid dealing with government departments or their officials who have two "mouths"; you cannot argue with them because you have only one mouth. Besides, the officials who saw the arrow in their work have also made life difficult for the illiterate and the poor. As inefficiency breeds corruption, countries which get rid of arrow-sawing government officials will become efficient, be more prosperous, and be respected for their good governance.

The Method of Mending the Pot (补 锅 法)

When the rice pot was leaking, a person was called to mend it. After scraping the bottom of the pot with an iron scraper, the man told the owner of the rice pot to go and get fire because he wanted to smoke. As the owner turned his back, the mender used a hammer to knock at the pot lightly to lengthen the existing crack. He then told the returning owner while pointing at the crack, "Your cooking pot has a long crack, it was covered with a layer of oil. The hidden crack could only be seen when the pot is scraped; more nails are needed for the repair work." The owner had a closer look at the crack; surprised, he said, "You are right! You are right! If I have not called you today, this pot could have become useless." When the pot was mended, both the owner and the mender were happy to part each other. (Liu Si 2005d: 21) Li commented that the two methods are interchangeable and can also be used simultaneously. Their applications in real life depend on how creative and imaginative the implementers are.

The Study of the Thin Face and the White Heart

Li's writings on *The Study of the Thick Face and the Black Heart* made him look like a rabid proponent who advocated that people must have thick skin and a black heart to succeed in life. Li met his match when his opponent introduced *The Study of the Thin Face and the White Heart* to signify that people must have a sense of shame and a pure heart before they could consider themselves to be an achiever in life. The irony turned out to be that the author of *The Study of the Thin Face and the White Heart* was himself found guilty of corruption and riding roughshod; he had to be beheaded. (Liu Si 2005e: 252) Li himself became a victim of his own doctrine, because he had to make sure that in whatever he did, he would not be accused of having a thick face and a black heart. This caused him to be so overly cautious that he couldn't do anything; it kept him from becoming a great man.

The world has become more materialistic, and the theory of *The Study of the Thin Face and the White Heart* has gradually come to mean being heartless and using "white silver," which means money. When you are heartless, which is worse than having a black heart, you become evil. When you use silver to bribe, the ancient Chinese saying has it that even the ghosts will do the grinding work for you. If you remember the milk powder scandal in China in September 2008, you will recall how thousands of babies had developed kidney stones from drinking milk made from toxic powder. The milk powder produced was contaminated with melamine, a chemical used in making plastics. Melamine has been illegally added to food products by the heartless people, who were concerned only with the white silver to increase their apparent protein content. Hence, when you apply the theories of *The Thick Face and the Black Heart* and that of the heartless and silver in your life, you are no more a human being. You become Satan personified.

Lessons to be Learnt from the Analogy of Han Feizi

Laozi, or the "Old Master," lived in the sixth century B.C. He was a philosopher and the centre figure of Daoism. On the other hand, Han Fei was a great thinker who called Laozi a wise man. Han Fei wrote *Han Feizi* to make clear the thinking of Laozi using his logical thinking, allegorically and convincingly.

Bian Que was a very famous and skilful physician among the people during the Warring States in China more than 2,000 years ago. Once, the crown prince of the emperor of an affiliated state had died of a sickness and was about to be buried. After having collected more information, Bian Que concluded that the crown prince was still alive and stood a chance to be saved.

Bian Que then revived the crown prince from his unconsciousness through the use of acupuncture, followed by applying medicine underneath his ribs to make him stand up; he made up a prescription for the crown prince to drink for about a month, after which the crown prince was totally cured of his sickness. However, it was puzzling that the father of the crown prince, the sick Emperor Cai Huan Gong, did not believe in Bian Que, who told him about his failing health on many occasions.

The following is the excerpt of the passage "Bian Que Meeting Cai Huan Gong," as contained in the book *Han Feizi Yu Lao* (Wuweixiaozi 2008):

> Bian Que called to pay respects to emperor Cai Huan and after a while said, "The skin of your Highness doesn't look healthy and if it is not treated, the disease may go into your body." Emperor Huan said, "I am not sick." After Bian Que had left, the emperor said, "Doctors like to treat people who are not sick to take credit for themselves."
>
> Ten days later, Bian Que paid a formal visit to the emperor again during which he said, "Your sickness had gone into your body and if it is not treated, I am afraid the disease will go further into your body." The emperor was not bothered and was not at all happy with Bian Que.
>
> Ten days later, Bian Que went to see the emperor again and told him, "Your sickness has now

affected your stomach and if no treatment is sought immediately, I am afraid the disease will continue to go deep into your body." Emperor Huan again paid no attention to the words of Bian Que who then left. After another ten days, Bian Que went to the emperor again but left immediately after seeing him. The emperor quickly sent his messenger to find out the reason why Bian Que had to leave so hurriedly.

Bian Que said, "When the disease was at the surface of the skin, it could be cured when some hot herbal medicines were placed on the affected spot and then bandaged with a piece of cloth; when the disease had gone into the skin, suffice it to use silver or stone needles to pierce at the strategic points of the nerve system; when the stomach was affected, a mixture of various herbs of which their essence could be easily absorbed by the intestines could still cure; when the disease had gone into the bone marrows, then there was no more way out. Now that the emperor's bone marrows had been affected, it would be useless for me to see him anymore." After five days, the emperor had pains all over his body but Bian Que was no way to be found to go and cure the emperor who soon died.

Hence a good physician will take a preemptive action to cure the skin when it shows an initial sign of being infected. The fight with the disease is of a small scale at this juncture. Similarly, the misfortune and the blessing of an event can also be detected at their superficial levels. Therefore it is said that "the wise man chooses to address all issues at the initial stage."

The analogy of not letting your health become aggravated can be applied to other aspects of your life. The nub of the argument is that when you face an imminent disaster, try to deal with it while it is still easy to manage; if you want to embark on a great task of prime importance, begin with its minute details.

The moral of this story is that when you are ill, see the doctor as soon as possible. Before your health gets worse, nip it in the bud. The death of Emperor Huan was due to his unrealistic self-confidence and his refusal to accept advice and help from Bian Que, the highly skilled physician. As prevention is better than cure, you must take precaution to preempt problems.

In solving social, cultural, economical, and political issues of a country, the authority must be proactive and have the wisdom to address the issues before they get out of control. Nothing should be swept under the carpet, thinking that problems can be solved by themselves; that will compound the problem. No assumption should be made that everyone will be law-abiding. The milk powder scandal in China serves as a good case study. Though a multidepartment investigation into the scandal was launched after the incident, it was too late for the unfortunate babies, because the "sickness" in the overall administration was allowed to seep into the country's bone marrow.

When inspection exemptions were previously granted to food producers, it was taken for granted that all safety regulations would be observed by the parties concerned. No one remembered Li's warnings of *The Thick Face and the Black Heart*, let alone the emergence of the heartless and the magic of white silver imbued in those who had weak character. Sometimes lessons can be learnt through mistakes, but other times, the mistakes are too costly.

I shall conclude this chapter with a Chinese saying: "While you should not have the heart to do people great harm, it is imperative that you should have the heart to guard against them." You are not to practise *The Thick Face and the Black Heart* but must be aware of its existence.

Summary

This chapter begins with the introduction of a famous Chinese book, *The Thick Face and the Black Heart,* which was written by Li Zhongwu and published in 1912; Li's book touched on the two main weaknesses of human nature: thick-skinned and black-hearted. By chance, Li discovered that the historical Chinese heroes possessed those two traits to become leaders, much to the chagrin of many historians.

Li sarcastically revealed his secret recipe of twelve genuine words and two brilliant methods to those who aspired to be government officials. The first six genuine words are for the begging of a government post: free, drilling, boasting, flattering, threatening, and giving; the next six genuine words are for serving government officials to amass their ill-gotten wealth: empty, servile, looking displeased, fierce, deaf, and amassing; and the two brilliant methods, sawing the arrow and mending the pot, are for officials to shirk their duties and yet seem to be diligently working.

Another book was written in response to Li's: *The Study of the Thin Face and the White Heart* was written by his opponent to disseminate the idea of a humane society. Ironically, the author was later beheaded for corruption, and this prompted Li to further insist that his book was relevant to all mankind.

The analogy of Han Feizi is manifested through Bian Que, an experienced physician. His advice to cure the emperor of his illness at its initial stages was not taken, resulting in the death of the emperor; it is to warn us that the symptoms in social-economic problems of a nation must be solved early before they become too difficult to address. This chapter therefore aims to expose you to the thick-faced and the black-hearted people you are very likely to meet in life. You are not to fall into the pitfall of being unscrupulous but flee to look beyond your horizon.

Chapter Two

The Two Most Important Persons in Your Life

The whole year's work depends on a good start at the beginning of the year. As time and tide wait for no man, it is always to your advantage that you start planning your future when you are young. You may not know what you want to be when you grow up; perhaps no one has given you any advice. You may not know whether your first job is suitable for you, because you have not yet been exposed to other alternative careers. You may be at a loss as what to do next other than living from day to day, like a boat without a rudder, drifting aimlessly in water.

What is missing in spurring you on is the advice on setting and planning your goals. When you fail to plan, you plan to fail. The pertinent question which you need to ask yourself is whether you are heading for the right direction in life. Are you like the proverbial blind mice, running down the alleyways without any aim but leaving everything to intuition? You have to chart your own future based on what you clearly want in life and truly believe that under all circumstances, you can achieve your goals.

As procrastination is a common human weakness, I would suggest that you go to your writing table, take out a piece of paper, and start writing down all your dreams. Put in writing all the things that you want to achieve in life. It does not matter if your dreams are wishful thinking; they may be difficult to materialise. Since you are alone in your study, think and write (longhand or on your computer) as if you are a roc and want to exploit your potential to the fullest.

The First Person You Must Know: Yourself

There are two keys to success in setting and planning your goals. *The Art of War* was written two thousand years ago by Sunzi, the greatest strategist in warfare in ancient China; one of its strategies was to know yourself. You need to know yourself and know yourself thoroughly.

To know yourself, you must evaluate your strengths and your weaknesses, your aptitude, and your innate talent. You need to know the theory of multiple intelligences, as first propounded by Howard Gardner, the famous American educator, in 1983. They are all in you, albeit of a different degree. Try to figure out whether you are word smart, logic smart, self-smart, music smart, spatial-visual smart, body smart, nature smart, people smart, or wondering smart. You should be excellent in one, two, or more of these intelligences (and good in several others).

Professor Roger Sperry (who won the Nobel Prize in medicine 1983) asserted that a person's brain can be divided into two: the left and the right hemispheres process information differently. That explains why you learn differently as compared to your friends. When you use both sides of your brain to study, think, and play, you also strengthen the less dominant hemisphere of the brain to learn effectively. You need to do what the two eminent professors said: know yourself better. They have widened the body of our knowledge in this field, allowing us to know ourselves better.

Know What You Are Good At

As you are in control of yourself, you should know what you are good at. You need to know your strengths, which can give you an edge over others, and take steps to improve on your weaknesses. Find out what you are capable of doing, and then you can start planning to reach your great potential with utmost confidence.

If you enjoy reading and have a flair for writing, you are a linguistically intelligent person. You are good at conveying to others your thoughts and feelings in a clear, orderly, and concise manner. You are suited for courses in mass communications, law, and teacher training. You will also make a good politician, writer, editor, novelist, public speaker, or religious leader because of your verbal and linguistic skills. You are more likely to be the one who sweeps all the prizes for literary and debate competitions in school, and the person who stands up to be counted when it comes to public speaking.

I now recall having a secondary schoolmate who was seen reading books almost all the time; he did not seem to study hard but always did well in examinations. When I met him a few years prior to our retirement, he was the English editor of a government news agency. He was definitely the right person to hold the job because of his mastery of the language.

When you consistently score high marks in mathematics, you are logic smart. Mathematics involves a great amount of critical and logical thinking. You must then have the ability to understand numbers, logical concepts, and patterns. Generally, when you are good in mathematics, you also excel in the science subjects that also involve numerous theorems and formulae. In the present digital world, a good knowledge of mathematics and science will enable you to become a competent computer programmer, scientist, banker, financial controller, entrepreneur, judge, detective, or accountant.

If you are good in both languages and mathematics, you tend to do well in school. A good mastery of languages enables you to understand and analyse literary works or lessons well, and a strong foundation in mathematics is the key to doing exceptionally well in science subjects. In the early 1950s and 1960s, primary school pupils in Taiwan only learned three subjects: languages, mathematics, and general science. Indeed, when you are good in languages and in mathematics, your dream of becoming a high achiever in any field of your choice is already assured.

A self-smart person is one who has good intrapersonal intelligence. You truly know yourself in and out when you possess this intelligence. You know what you want and what you are capable of achieving in life. You are very sure of your goals in life. If you belong to this category of people, then planning for your future becomes an easy task. You need not have to take up courses which your parents have no opportunity to study or be what they want you to be and not what you want yourself to be. When you understand that your talent is infinite, you will be highly motivated. You are already halfway to success when you know yourself thoroughly. Sunzi said it two thousand years ago, and it is still very much relevant today: When you know yourself, half the battle is won. As a self-smart person, you can work independently and with commitment. You will be comfortable working as a psychologist or a psychiatrist or in some other career you enjoy.

If you love and enjoy music, then you are music smart, and a career in music will suit you well. Even if you do not take up music as your career, your love for music indicates that you may live a gracious and happy life. I envy those who have musical intelligence. It may interest you to know that Albert Einstein, the scientist behind the world's most famous equation, $E = mc^2$, was a great lover of music, and he also played the violin. When asked to define the meaning of death, Einstein replied by saying that it meant he would never again be able to enjoy the beautiful music of Mozart.

B. F. Skinner was an American psychologist, author, inventor, and social philosopher who also enjoyed music. He had a ritual of playing all of Mozart's sonatas all the way through, once a year. So if you love and enjoy music, count it as a great blessing. Sing and dance with the music and enjoy the rhythmic pace of life. Music helps to develop the right hemisphere of your brain to make you creative and imaginative, so cultivate your love for music. Life will be so invigorating and happier with music around you. You can also develop an appreciation of music to de-stress and gain a cheerful disposition.

When I was in school, I had a phobia about drawing; I could not draw a simple object during art lessons. I was not visual smart and lacked spatial-visual intelligence. If you are sensitive to the inter-relationship between line, shape, space, form, and colour, you should be glad that you have been endowed with this spatial-visual intelligence. The digital world needs talented people like you to help them in graphic arts and in creating three-dimensional images. If you have always enjoyed playing chess, be assured that it has helped you tremendously, without you realising it, in enhancing this intelligence of yours. If you are not sure of what you want to be when you grow up but you have this spatial-visual intelligence, then you can choose to be a painter, engineer, artist, sculptor, photographer, navigator, pilot, florist, dancer, or architect. You know how to appreciate beauty and art.

When you are asked to name your former schoolmates of ten or twenty years ago, you are likely to remember those who excelled in sports and are body smart. You remember the house captains or team captains or the players who brought glory to the school. If you are active in sports and co-curricular activities, you have bodily-kinesthetic intelligence. If you know how to plan your time between sports and study, you are also very likely to do well academically.

By being active in sports, you are fit physically and have enough oxygen in you to make you alert. As sports help to activate the right hemisphere of your brain, you become more creative and imaginative than those who shy away from outdoor activities.

You need to be innovative and intuitive to play games well. When you apply this in your study or work, you become an effective learner and performer. If you are also born a dancer, then you can move with grace, and this is a gift for having the bodily-kinesthetic intelligence. You have fine-motor coordination and can become a surgeon, gymnast, dancer, jeweler, physical therapist, or athlete.

Since you have learnt to have team spirit, you are inevitably good in interpersonal skill and become a leader. This will help you to a great extent in your career. You will be the leader of your organisation. Therefore, take time off to exercise and engage yourself actively in outdoor activities to keep physically fit and mentally strong. Those who spend too much time watching sporting events on television are at most passive sportsmen. Go out to the field and enjoy yourself. It is both refreshing and benefiting to your health. And remember: leaders generally come from the field not from the classroom.

The ancient Chinese talked about the five elements in nature: metal, wood, water, fire, and earth. These were held by the ancients to represent the physical universe; later, they were used in traditional Chinese medicine to explain various physiological and pathological phenomena. The ancient Greeks, on the other hand, believed there were four elements: earth, air, fire, and water. They were manifestations of an underlying primal substance: goat. (Ancient Greek Philosophers 2008) Both civilisations therefore touched on things that were of nature.

Do you like planting, gardening, mountain climbing, camping, marathon running, swimming, studying biology or botany, or caring for pets? Are you concerned about the environmental issues that are plaguing the world? Do you need to have your workplace clean and free of rubbish on the floor? Do you want your surroundings filled with more trees and plants? If so, then you are nature smart.

Hence, you tend to love nature and are interested in plant, bird, fish, and animal species. As a protector of the environment and nature, your favourite outdoor activities are related to mountains, sea, rivers, parks, and other natural settings. I should love to visit your home because it will likely be tastefully decorated with beautiful garden, plants, and flowers. Your house is not likely to be a mess but cosy. The right hemisphere of your brain is so creative that visitors to your home are likely to over-stay their welcome. If you are good in naturalist intelligence, you should consider becoming a botanist, zoologist, interior designer, veterinarian, or even an astronomer.

Are you popular among your friends or colleagues? Do you enjoy social gatherings? Do you have empathy—the ability to imagine yourself in the position of your friends, and so understand their feelings? Do you refrain from using your i-Phone, i-Pad, or other digital gadgets during social gatherings? If so, then you have the interpersonal intelligence to be people smart. Your friends will feel at ease talking to you, and they like to be your friends because you respect them. You are very likely to be a leader and a good listener.

At this juncture, I will share with you a Chinese classical joke: "Great Liu Hosting a Feast."

Great Liu was poor in communication skills and so had offended many people without him knowing why. On his fiftieth birthday, he invited his friends: Zhang Three, Li Four, Wang Five, and Zhao Six, for a gathering and to entertain them at the feast. When the feast was about to be served, Zhao Six was the only one who had not arrived. Great Liu was visibly upset and said, "The one who should come is not here." After hearing this, Zhang Three thought, *I might be the one who shouldn't come.* So he left the party.

Great Liu, on seeing Zhang Three leaving, then hurriedly said, "Ah! The one who shouldn't go has gone." Li Four was not happy with this statement, which he thought insinuated that he should be the one to go. Without any hesitation, he left immediately.

When Li Four left, Great Liu shook his head and said to Wang Five, "I didn't mean him." Wang Five was hurt, and a thought came to his mind: *If you are not referring to him, you must be telling me off.* He then rose and departed from the house. With a dull look in his eyes, Great Liu uttered helplessly, "What have I said? Why did they leave?" (Classical Jokes 2008)

On the other hand, generally, when you are body smart, you are also people smart. This is so because when you play basketball, football, netball, or hockey, you know your team cannot win all the time. You learn to accept defeat graciously and do not blame other players for it. As you learn to have team spirit, you know that no man is an island and you need the co-operation of friends to be successful in life.

When you are people smart, you also possess the emotional intelligence (EI) to interact well with others. EI is often measured as an emotional intelligence quotient (EQ), and it is what makes you popular as a leader. If you look around you, you are likely to realise that generally people with high intelligence quotients (IQs) are working for people with high EQs, other factors remaining constant. When you have a high EQ and are people smart, you are more flexible in dealing with others. You will notice that when you are people smart, you can get things done easier and faster. If you are people smart, you can become a politician, actor, sociologist, human resource executive, salesperson, personal consultant, nurse, or TV talk show host.

Are you inquisitive and always question the meaning of life and death? Do you wonder why are we born, why people die, why people suffer from chronic diseases? Do you always ponder on the realities of living in this world? You may ask a series of questions to learn why people hurry to chase after material comfort at the expense of their health.

Confucius, the philosopher and scholar, wanted to know what the truth was. He even said that he was willing to die in the evening if he could hear the truth in the morning. Confucius, together with Socrates, Plato, and Aristotle, are examples of people who are wondering smart. They always ask why. This is the existential intelligence mentioned by Gardner. It is also called cosmic smart, spiritual smart, and meta-physical intelligence. If you are wondering smart dominant, you can be a good preacher or philosopher.

You may now be more convinced than ever why you are better in the arts or in the sciences, why you are an introvert or an extrovert. You have come to know yourself better and have a good appraisal of yourself. This wisdom of knowing yourself is vital to achieve your far-reaching aspirations. You have become much more knowledgeable about yourself and knowing what you are good at. If you have been ignorant of your talent and potential before, *now* is the time for you to take steps to change from a finch to a roc and look beyond your horizon.

Your Biological Rhythms

Your negativity in life may also be overcome if you know your biorhythms and maximise their use. Adjust your work schedules accordingly and start afresh. If this is not possible because of the nature of your work, then you may have to change your lifestyle with a new biological clock. You have to be flexible enough to cope with life in the fast changing world. After Thomas Edison invented electricity, people began to sleep late at night but have to wake up early to work. However, Edison, who slept for less than four hours a night, maintained that the opportunity cost was high when too much time was spent sleeping and it was "a deplorable regression to the primitive state of a caveman." Nevertheless, he napped to make up for his short sleep at night.

Napoleon Bonaparte, whose name starts with "Nap," napped because he was a chronic insomniac and could only sleep about three hours a night. Albert Einstein took a daily naps to refresh his mind and make him more creative. Other personalities who napped frequently were Winston Churchill and Presidents Kennedy, Reagan, and Clinton. (Power Sleep: 2008) Legend has it that Leonardo da Vinci (1452-1519), the great Italian artist who painted the masterpiece *Mona Lisa,* only slept for ninety minutes a day; he napped for fifteen minutes every four hours. (Google 2008b) You should know your own biological rhythms and adjust your sleeping hours accordingly. Catnapping, however, is highly recommended to recharge your energy.

When you know yourself well, you can get twice the result with half the effort if you work according to your plan. You are to know that if you repeatedly do the same thing using the same method, you will get the same results. For example, are you always rushing for time? If so, then you must try to find out the blind spot that makes you on the run all the time. Plan your work day and use your time wisely. You can have a good breakfast if you go to sleep early and wake up early; this way, you can sit at the dining table and enjoy your breakfast, which you should prepare the night before. If you leave your house twenty to thirty minutes earlier than others, after having a good breakfast, you will be in a happy mood and not be anxious about traffic jams and being late for work. You can also think over your plan for the day. If you are using public transport, you can make use of the transit time to read. If you were to accumulate the reading time while in transit, you will marvel at the number of books you could have read and the enormous knowledge that could have entered your mind at the end of each year.

I know of two friends who work in the same publishing company; this firm allows its staff to work flexible hours, according to their own preferred biological rhythms, to obtain maximum efficiency. One of them starts work at 7.30 a.m. and goes home early, while the other reaches the office at 11.00 a.m. and returns home late. The flexible working hours make both of them happy, thereby increasing their productivity. If you do not enjoy such a privilege and have to work from nine-to-five, you should do the most difficult or important task at the time when your biorhythms best suit you. You are not likely to be at a high productivity level after lunch. Hence, you should take a short break after lunch to relax and get your blood circulating again.

Paulo Coelho

Paulo Coelho (1947-present) is one of the world's best loved storytellers. He is a Brazilian writer whose translated books have been widely published. He is a publishing phenomenon whose visionary writing can change your life and inspire you to fly like a roc and look beyond your horizon. Go to the Internet or a bookshop and order some of his books. You will surely be enlightened in many aspects of knowing yourself. I would recommend you read *The Alchemist,* which has sold over thirty-five million books worldwide and has been translated into sixty-three languages. (Coelho 2002)

Alchemists in the Middle Ages tried to turn different metals into gold and sought medicines to cure all diseases. The term is now used to signify a person who has the potential to turn a common thing into something unusual and precious. Hence, the theme of Coelho's book is that we have the capability to change our dream into reality while sojourning in this world.

The story begins with Santiago, a shepherd boy who aspires to tour round the world in search of his treasure. After telling a gypsy woman of this dream, he is told to follow his dream. Santiago finally sets off for Egypt, only to have a fateful encounter with an alchemist. Santiago falls in love with a girl named Fatima, whose desert tribe was fighting a war with the other tribes. He went to the Pyramids and realised that the treasure he had been searching for was Fatima.

This shows that love never fails. When love abounds, life becomes meaningful. It also manifests to you that when you know yourself thoroughly, you can follow your dream of what you love to do, and your dream will come true one day. This was exactly what Coelho had done when he was fifteen years old. At that time, he had already made up his mind to be a writer, against the wishes of his mother, who wanted him to be an engineer like his father or a doctor like his uncle. (Google 2008b) Therefore, the first person you need to know to be successful in life is yourself. As I have said, when you know yourself, you are already halfway to success. You can avoid taking up courses that you do not like or do not have the aptitude to do well. When you choose your career, you will select one that you love and enjoy doing. You are to achieve your own personal goals and not necessarily the goals of your parents. Choose a career and not a job.

Now that you know yourself thoroughly, you should meet the second person who can decide whether you will ultimately be a high achiever in life or not.

The Second Person You Must Know: Your Enemy

Your negativity is your enemy.

You must always remember that your negativity can soon dampen your initial enthusiasm and that of others. For example, one furious act of yours can negate all the peace-making efforts of your friends. Hence, when we talk about knowing your enemy, we are not talking about your physical enemy in the battlefield. Your enemy is your own self. Your enemy, the second person you need to know, can be in the form of lack of self-confidence, selfishness, laziness, procrastination, greediness, pessimism, arrogance, apathy, jealousy, unforgiving, rudeness, unfriendliness, dishonesty, spendthrift, or untidiness. It can also be in the form of the thick face and the black heart. If you want to overcome these weaknesses, then you have to take steps to overcome them. You are on the right track when you begin to have a paradigm shift and think outside the box.

You can overcome your negativity by developing good character and possessing a positive attitude and self-confidence; this will command respect from your friends. To do so, you must nurture yourself in character building.

Character Building

There once was a man who carved a mulberry leaf out of jade for the king. It took him three years to complete the project. The craftsmanship was so superb that the finished product looked just like a leaf. When placed among real mulberry leaves, it was indistinguishable from the real ones. From then on, the man lived on his skills in the state.

When Liezi, a thinker in ancient China two thousand years ago, heard about this, he said, "If it has to take three years for nature to produce a single leaf, then there would be too few trees with leaves! Hence, what sages and men of virtue rely on are the moral teachings and not the craftiness of wisdom." (Baidu-E 2008) Liezi put morality before wisdom. A moral education, or character building, is more important than someone's resourcefulness or wisdom.

At the age of sixteen, Zengzi (505-436 BC) was under the tutelage of Confucius, who did not consider him to be intelligent. However, Confucius praised him for being very diligent in his studies. Zengzi was very particular about practising what you preach and proposed that a person should examine himself on three aspects every day as a guide towards character building. He suggested that we should ask ourselves these three questions: Have I helped others with all my heart? Have I been truthful to my friends? Have I revised the lessons that have been taught to me? If there is any shortcoming, correct it, and if there is none, further encourage yourself. (Baidu 2013a)

Zengzi's view on character building therefore propagates kindness, honesty, and a desire to learn. Indeed, you will be respected when you walk the talk, meaning what you say and doing what you mean. As a trustworthy person, you must keep your promises. It is said that a picture is worth a thousand words and an example is worth a thousand pictures. Furthermore, examples are caught and not taught.

You are therefore reminded to earnestly practise what you advocate, because others judge you based on what you do and say. Your friends will be touched by your compassion and trust you for your truthfulness. As it is getting more difficult to find people who are sincere and keep their promises in this materialistic world, your sincerity in dealing with people will be an added advantage in all your endeavours. Others will then take a leaf out of your book as regards integrity.

Confucius, the great philosopher and educator in ancient China, said, "Study as if time is running short; learn just in case you may lose what you have acquired." To become a high achiever, you must always be eager to learn and improve yourself. Confucius said that when he was fifteen years old, he had already set his goal to learn and to build his character. At the age of thirty, he was independent. At the age of forty, he understood many things. By the time he was fifty, he was able to see clearly the complexities in the universe. At sixty, he understood whatever he had heard, and at seventy, he could do whatever he wished to without overdoing things. (Chen 1966: 308)

You should emulate this goal of lifelong learning. When you set your goal to learn, you are heading for success. Remember that a little drop can become a mighty ocean one day. You are building a firm foundation to excel in life, because knowledge is power. When you learn, you also learn of the good traits found in successful people and try to emulate them. If you examine yourself daily on this aspect, you will find that through revision and restudying old material, you will gain new insights.

Learn to Learn under All Circumstances

There is a Chinese saying which literally means "enough books to make the ox carrying them sweat." This is similar to having an immense number of books to fill a house to the rafters. With the advent of the Internet, the amount of reading material can figuratively fill the air. Thus, you are at the threshold of a vast accumulation of both ancient and present literature for you to explore. Use your time wisely to venture into the world of knowledge.

Remember that your success in life depends partly on your talent, eagerness to learn, and your effort and partly on your opportunity. Your opportunity is the combination of timeliness, favourable environment, and support of people. You are advantaged to be at your age in quest of knowledge, which can now be acquired easily. The sky is the limit for you to learn as much as you want to. You were born at the right time to reap the benefits of digital inventions. The environment for learning is excellent because of the ease of travel and the availability of resource centres, i-Pads, i-Phones, laptops, and computers. Besides, you have all the learned people around you easily available to be your mentors in teaching you the finesse in life. All you need to do is ask, and ask humbly.

A workman must first sharpen his tools if he is to do his work well. Similarly, if you want to do well in your study or career, you have to first sharpen your tools. What are your tools that need sharpening? They are firstly your mastery of languages, and secondly your power of critical thinking. When you revise the lessons that have been taught to you, you inculcate an interest in learning. Besides learning, you must also read. This is the only way to sharpen your tool of languages. A person who reads today is a leader tomorrow. When you make reading your daily habit, your mind will gradually be enlightened and reach its peak. Confucius said that if a person did not read books for three days, he would be repulsive in appearance.

When you are bilingual, trilingual, or even multilingual in this globalised world, you will definitely stand out in your career over those who are monolingual. When you know more than one language, your horizon is widened because you have access to many different worlds and cultures. This will help you to look at things from various perspectives and nurture you to be critical in your thinking. Your life will be so much more colourful and enriched when you are broad-minded, understanding, and compassionate and accept the fact that there can be unity in diversity.

If you are also proactive, accommodating, and optimistic, others will admire your virtues. Therefore, be inspired and master at least two languages, including the English language, to look beyond your horizon. Go and bury yourself in the wonderful world of timeless stories to sharpen your tool of languages and the power of critical thinking. Your eagerness in learning begins with reading, which helps to develop your reasoning ability. In fact, when you keep learning things that you enjoy, you are activating your brain. Always remember that an idle mind is the workplace of the devil, whose name is Alzheimer.

The Love of Money Is the Root of All Evil

Greediness is a great enemy to most people. The downfall of a country can be due to the corrupt leaders and officials who rapaciously plunder the resources of their country, without compunction. If you can overcome this temptation, you will do well in life. It is important for you to shun evil deeds, like taking bribes, or go against your conscience to amass ill-gotten wealth. You should also not cheat others of their hard-earned money or bring shame to yourself and your family. Mengzi said, "A person cannot be without a sense of shame. If he thinks it shameful not to have it, then he will never experience shame throughout his life." You should avoid unethical conduct to make sure you do not bring disgrace to yourself, your family, your beliefs, and your community.

In order to overcome your enemy, character building must be your top priority in life. With a sense of shame, you will fear God and obey the laws of the country. Marcus Aurelius (AD 121-180), a Roman emperor for almost twenty years, said, "The happiness of your life depends on the quality of your thoughts: therefore, guard accordingly, and take care that you entertain no notions unsuitable to virtue and reasonable nature." Therefore, think and act positively to overcome the evil forces in you.

When you regard laziness, deceiving your friends, dependency on others, reaping profits without toiling, jealousy, and other negative traits as shameful, then you have come to know your enemy. To overcome your enemy, you will then work hard, stand on your own two feet, toil diligently to reap your harvest, be compassionate, and inculcate only good habits. You will then not blame others for your failure. In doing so, you will not only be respected for what you are but also achieve great successes in life. Those with a sense of shame also have honour, self-esteem, and responsibility. When you stand straight, you are not afraid of your shadow being crooked.

Always remember that your achievement is not measured solely from the aspects of your academic, marketing, administrative, or job performances, but also on your integrity. Life without values is meaningless. When you are both literate and educated, you can overcome your enemy with your positive values. Aristotle, a great thinker of ancient Greece, said, "Educating the mind without educating the heart is no education at all." Have a compassionate heart and your enemy will flee from you.

Gandhi was famous for being kind and compassionate. One day as he stepped aboard a train, one of his shoes slipped off and landed on the track. He could not retrieve it since the train was moving. To the astonishment of his friends, Gandhi calmly removed his other shoe and threw it back along the track, close to the first. When asked for the reason of doing so, Gandhi smiled and said gently, "The poor man who finds the shoes lying on the track will now have a pair he can use."

It will be magnanimous of you to manifest your generous qualities towards others, beyond what is usual or necessary, as narrated in the following Native American story.

The Two Wolves

In this Cherokee tale, a grandfather was telling his grandson about a fight between two wolves that was going on in his heart. He said, "One is evil: anger, envy, sorrow, regret, fearful thinking, greed, arrogance, self-pity, guilt, resentment, inferiority, lies, false pride, superiority, and ego. The other wolf is good: joy, peace, love, hope, serenity, humility, kindness, benevolence, empathy, generosity, truth, compassion, and faith." The grandson thought about this for a minute and then asked his grandfather, "Which wolf wins?" "The one I feed," the grandfather answered. (AAA Native Arts 2002-2008)

There may be a similar dilemma within your heart now. What should you do in order to fly like a roc, knowing that the sky is your limit as a high achiever? Feed the one which has love, because love never fails. When you give more than you receive, it shows that you are not selfish but generous. You will have all the virtues with you. Therefore know who your enemies are and shun them.

Incidentally, the Cherokee are a Native American people who previously lived in the Appalachian Mountains; present-day populations live in northern Oklahoma and western North Carolina. The Cherokee were removed to Indian Territory in the 1830s following conflicts with American settlers over rights to their traditional lands.

The Four Advisory Notes

In life, you are encouraged to compete with your own self rather than with other people. Always ask: Am I better prepared for life today as compared to yesterday? Am I moving forward as days go by? Am I optimistic and confident in doing things? Have I equipped myself to face the challenges in the ever-changing world? Am I happy with my career?

I shall now touch on four areas you should observe in order to succeed.

1) Know when to implement your plan

If your plan is not well prepared, do not implement it, for it will be a failure if you do so. For example, if you have not prepared yourself fully for an examination, you will surely fail. You should not then have registered yourself for the examination in the first place. You must know when it is the right time to both register and sit for the examination. Once you have done so, prepare yourself for the battle, which can and must be won.

If you have a presentation to do at your office, you know yourself whether you are ready to do so or not. If you are not prepared for it, or if you have not put in any effort to do a good job out of it, then it is better for you to postpone it than to end in disgrace. Identify and get rid of your enemy, which can be in the form of incompetence or lack of enthusiasm. Learn to equip yourself first.

2) Know for sure which wolf you are feeding

Now that you have determined the two very important persons in your life, you can go through all the multiple intelligences again and write down those that are more dominant and those that are less dominant in you. You should also list all your weaknesses and treat them collectively as your enemy. You are to make plans to overcome them. When you plan, make a visionary plan and look ahead in time. Your goals should be in harmony with humanity, with society, with nature, and most important of all with your heart and mind.

When you have all your perspectives and principles simultaneously positioned correctly, you can then go and implement your plan with a good conscience, giving no room for resentment later on. This calls for you to examine the three aspects in your life every day, all of which you have just learnt. Ultimately the crux of the matter is, Which of the two wolves are you allied with?

3) Individual strength and teamwork

In the networking world, no one is an island. You may be a born leader, but you still need the cooperation of your colleagues. Your individual strengths, like leadership traits, are a boon to the organisation if you exploit them to the fullest. For example, if you are captain of a football team, all the players on the field need to play as a team under your command. The team cannot win without an experienced captain, relying solely on the individual skills of one or two players. This analogy can be applied to any organisation that you are heading.

You must always remember that the synergy obtained from combining your individual talent and the power of teamwork is more effective than the sum of their separate efforts. This is so because the cohesiveness, the abundance of innovative ideas, and the sharing of responsibility in teamwork will ensure your success in life.

4) Recruit not the one you doubt; doubt not the one you recruit

There is an old Chinese saying that a commander in chief must use acumen to select his team of high ranking officers, while the latter must have the sharpness of mind to recruit junior officers and men. The analogy is that the prime minister of a country must have the ability to judge well in selecting his cabinet ministers, while the latter must use shrewdness when appointing department heads. In modern management, the CEO must be able to identify managers who are an asset to the company, while the latter use their strength to recruit good supporting staff. When you look around at the chaotic situation of Third World countries and developing economies, you will know the wisdom of this old saying.

If you are given the mandate to hire and fire, it is vital that you do not recruit anyone whose suitability to the job is in doubt; you should also not doubt the ability of the staff you have recruited. When you delegate work, manifesting your trust in the staff will motivate them to further contribute to the organisation. Hence, when you are given the authority to head a section, it is your duty to guide and motivate. Constant interference, however, will annoy those below you. To prove my point that it is better for you to trust your subordinates, let me relate the story of a rich man whose judgement was not right.

There was a rich man in the state of Song in ancient China, whose wall was ruined by heavy rain. His son said, "If this wall is not repaired now, thieves will surely come and steal our things." His neighbour's father said the same thing. True enough, the house was broken into at night, and many things were stolen. The rich man thought that the boy was clever, but he was suspicious that his neighbour could be the culprit. This is the source of the idiom "Rain ruined the wall" and "The man of Song suspects his neighbour." When two people say the same thing, you may tend to think well of what a person says and suspect the words spoken by the other person out of prejudice. The moral is that it is not easy for us to pass value judgement based on the facts given. (Baidu-D 2008)

When you are at the management level, allow your subordinates to show that they are capable of making the grade and excel in their performances. Let them take pride in their work. Those who work in an environment when their talent is not doubted will always try hard to prove their worth. What is important is that you must be a trustworthy and capable leader in the first place. Thus, when you know yourself and your enemy, and remember the four advisory notes, you will be victorious in all the battles that you engage in.

Summary

Sunzi's two-thousand-year-old book of strategy, *The Art of War*, stresses, among many other things, the two persons whom you must know in order to succeed in life: yourself and your enemy. You should know your multiple intelligences and whether you are left-brain-dominant or right-brain-dominant. Only then can you choose a career best suited to your aptitude. The importance of having emotional intelligence is mirrored in the classical Chinese story, "Great Liu Hosting a Feast." Learning about biological rhythms can help you know the importance of adjusting your best working hours to get twice the result with half the effort. You should also learn from Paulo Coelho, one of the world's most admired storytellers, who knew exactly what he wanted in life.

Your negativity is your enemy and the second person you must thoroughly know. Your enemy can be the thick face and the black-hearted personified. Hence, if you can overcome your weaknesses, you will become proactive, optimistic, and confident and possess a good character that will help make you a successful person in life. You are advised to study under all circumstances to improve your worth in the job market and know that the love of money is the root of all evil. Of the two wolves in your heart, you should choose to feed the good wolf, which abounds in love. This chapter also offers you the four advisory notes which can help you to look beyond your horizon: know when to execute your plan; be sure to feed the good wolf; use both individual strength and teamwork; and trust and delegate: do not doubt the person you have recruited.

Chapter Three

Take a Broad and Long-Term View in Life

When you take a broad and long-term view in life, you are far-sighted. A roc flying high in the sky can have a helicopter view of the ground below, while a finch's view is that of a peephole: narrow and limited. You think big because you stand high and see far; you think small because your ambition is inhibited by your lack of exposure and motivation. You can only widen your horizon when you are not blinded by your negativity and the thick face and the black heart.

When you use your past and present experiences to develop a future personal or business plan, you are a forward thinking person. You do not only see what is under your nose, like a mouse seeing only an inch away. When you stand high and look far, you distinguish yourself as a person with a very confident and cheerful disposition. Others will long to emulate your action.

Helen Adams Keller (1880-1968), the American writer, became deaf and blind when she was only nineteen months old, due to an illness. Though she could not hear, others lent her their ears; though she had lost her sight, she was not lacking in insight. Her enthusiasm in living a meaningful life despite her physical handicaps inspired many people to carry on living. Keller made life worth living by "standing high and seeing far," on her own accord. It was no wonder that Winston Churchill called her "the greatest woman of our age." Mark Twain said Keller and Napoleon were the two greatest characters in the nineteenth century. He said, "Napoleon tried to conquer the world by physical force, and failed. Helen tried to conquer the world by power of mind, and succeeded!" (Answers Corporation 2008)

The Enlightenment from Orwell's Books

At this juncture, I should like to introduce you to two of my favourite books, *Animal Farm* and *1984*. George Orwell had an almost flawless visualisation in writing them. If you read them, you may gain an insight into his critical thinking and vision. It is to be noted that "George Orwell" is only a pen name. The man behind these two classics was Eric Arthur Blair, who was born to a middle-class British family living in Bengal, India, in 1903.

The common theme in the novels *Animal Farm* and *1984* was Orwell's contempt for and fear of dictatorship. He argued that corrupt leaders should be removed from the world through the sanguine satire of the *Animal Farm* and the poverty and violence of *1984*. Orwell did not have a happy childhood because of the social chaos of the 1940s. When these books are revisited today, they become immediately relevant to us.

Animal Farm

In 1960, when I was in Form Two, my English literature teacher introduced me to *Animal Farm,* a popular novel which was first published in 1945 and was made into a film in 1955. This memorable fable tells the story of the revolution of the animals living on Manor Farm. A pig named Napoleon (a caricature of a French dictator) rose to become the leader of the farm. The farm was renamed "Animal Farm" after the farmer, a lazy and tyrannical drunkard, was forced to flee. I highly recommend you watch the movie, an animated cartoon.

Orwell's *Animal Farm* had seven rules of law. They were inscribed at a prominent place, above the door of a big barn, for the animals to remember and obey forever:

1. Whatever goes upon two legs is an enemy.
2. Whatever goes upon four legs or has wings is a friend.
3. No animal shall wear clothes.
4. No animal shall sleep in a bed.
5. No animal shall drink alcohol.
6. No animal shall kill another animal.
7. All animals are equal.

Later on, some rules were changed to read:

4. No animal shall sleep in a bed with sheets.
5. No animal shall drink alcohol in excess.
6. No animal shall kill another animal without reason.

The abridged version of the seven rules can be summed up as: "All animals are equal but some animals are more equal than others."

Ironically, in 2012, Bill Gates gave a speech at an American high school about the eleven rules of life students do not learn in school, with Rule No. 1 being "Life is not fair; get used to it!" You may pass your own critical and value judgements on this and as to whether all men are brothers in this world; are some men more equal than others?

1984

After writing *Animal Farm,* Orwell wrote the novel *1984,* which was published in 1949. Orwell was very visionary indeed when he said that the world of 1984 would witness the use of wars and conflicts to justify infringement on freedom; powerful media to distort facts and rewrite history; and tiny cameras to pry into private lives of others. He also predicted that after the year 1984, individuals would need to fight for their freedom of speech, freedom of expression, privacy, and life. Orwell's Big Brother is here today in the form of surveillance equipment and Internet search engines. They are reminiscent of an all-controlling power over our lives.

Does this ring a bell in you? It was a very different time when Orwell wrote the book, and yet he predicted with precision a future world governed by Big Brothers. Based on his experiences under the authoritative type of governance, Orwell's forecast was prophetic. In the modern world, as distinct from the time of the *Animal Farm,* knowledge is power, information is power, money is power, and state-of-the-art military equipment is power; we can't help bringing ourselves back to *1984.* Superpowers fulfilling all these criteria call all the shots.

From another perspective, it is common for some officials and public agency clerks to act like powerful little Napoleons. These warlords intimidate others and consolidate their power by means of craftiness. It is each on its own. Orwell's Napoleon, a boar, was the main tyrant of the *Animal Farm.* Napoleon was a coward who made use of vicious dogs as his secret agents and other animals to fight and die for the farm while he was busy building up his own empire. Remember the two brilliant methods of Li: sawing the arrow and mending the pot? Little Napoleons were experts in them.

When George Orwell wrote *1984,* the social-economic and politic state was very different from that of today. There was certainly no satellite TV, let alone the high-tech digital inventions of the present day. People today cannot live through a day without a smart phone, i-Pad, laptop, or computer. The knowledge-based Internet is frightening in its speed of change, complexity, functionality, and thoroughness. On second thought, could search engines ultimately be one of the all-controlling powers over our lives that Orwell warned us of? How are you going to make sure that you can cope with the changes when Big Brother shifts your goal post all the time?

The great demand on surveillance equipment has resulted in the surveillance industry being a growing and profitable business. Many governments are spending a sizeable amount of their budgets on CCTV surveillance at public areas to safeguard innocent citizens. CCTV has now become relevant to our daily life, and privacy will soon be a thing of the past. Many residential premises must be gated, and the residents have to pay their monthly subscriptions to engage security guards to look after their safety. Have you ever pondered that all these are unnecessary if people are taught to have character?

Orwell also mentioned that the whole literature of the past would have been destroyed. Chaucer, Shakespeare, Milton, and Byron, just to name a few, would exist only in "Newspeak" versions, resulting in a paradigm shift in the critical thinking of the people. (Bulletin Solutions 2003) The implication was that in an attempt to eliminate free thinking, the government of *1984* banned words that might encourage citizens to think for themselves. To digress, it is interesting to note that Emperor Qin Shi Huang, who built the Great Wall of China two thousand years ago, ordered all books to be burnt so that no one could be knowledgeable enough to go against him. He knew that the pen was mightier than the sword. Nevertheless, Emperor Qin, who failed to destroy all of China's literary works, has been credited for the emergence of the country's common written language.

Orwell's government of *1984* also introduced "Doublethink," which was a vast system of mental cheating. Ironically, the Ministry of Peace concerned itself with war, the Ministry of Truth with lies, the Ministry of Love with torture, and the Ministry of Plenty with starvation. These were to be deliberate exercises in Doublethink, which makes lies appear to be true. If you have been following the international news, through the mass media, YouTube, or the Internet, you may marvel at how intuitive and imaginative Orwell was.

However, when you tell the second lie to cover your first lie, and the third to cover your second, you will have an insurmountable task to convince others when it comes to the tenth lie, especially when information can be obtained and disseminated easily and quickly in the cyber world. Wouldn't it be better to call a spade a spade and just report the truth?

In *1984*, anyone suspected of acting against the government would be vaporised by the secret police. They would be arrested without charge and never heard from again. While the characters in 1984 were tracked by voice recognising microphones, you can now be spied on by state-of-the-art eavesdropping devices and through surveillance of web usage, email, phone logs, and fax records. You may also realise that your ID cards can now store information on names, addresses, fingerprints, and biometric information.

Today, there is a programme of online spying which knows no bounds; the Planning Tool for Resource Integration, Synchronisation, and Management (PRISM) is able to record millions of gigabytes every hour of emails, Twitter posts, videos, Skype conversations, and social networking posts. When you read *1984*, you will surely empathise with Orwell over his fears.

Orwell wrote many other books, amongst them a collection of short stories titled *Inside the Whale*. These very fine essays show Orwell at his best, discussing literature, recounting his experience in Burma, and commenting on Tolstoy's criticism of Shakespeare. These essays are a good read and wholly enjoyable. Read them to not only enlarge your body of knowledge but also provide a platform for more critical thinking.

When Can You Take a Broad and Long-Term View in Life?

Helen Keller once said, "One can never consent to creep when one feels an impulse to soar." This explains why Keller was well remembered for her sincere desire in doing the things she wanted in life despite of her handicaps. She never gave up and was a fighter with great confidence in herself and her own abilities. When Keller committed herself to get the best out of her life, she had already positioned herself to stand high and see far. So when can you take a broad and long-term view in life? It is when you manifest the following characteristics:

When You Are Forward-Looking

The new millennium in the twenty-first century offers you unparalleled possibilities to explore and attain whatever you set out to do. When you are forward-looking, you anticipate the future trends of your favourite subjects. Has George Orwell's literature given you an insight into some of your critical thoughts? Your wildest dreams can be made a reality because of the exponential growth of computer power. When I was at the university in the 1970s, computers were so bulky that one filled up an entire room; students had to line up to use it. It was then very expensive for the university to purchase one such computer. The invention of tiny chips has now reshaped and rechartered our destination in modern civilisation. Soon a microchip with today's processing power will just be the cost of scrap paper.

Everything in this world has the word "smart" attached to it: smart schools, smart cars, and the soon-to-be smart roads. Indeed, you will notice that every object in life, like TV sets, refrigerators, dishwashers, radios, digital gadgets, and laptops, involves ubiquitous computing. If you are computer literate, you are part of the modern world. The computers of the future will go even deeper into the very fabric of your life. "You are wonderfully young!" That was how an eighty-year-old elder described me when I was fifty. In the eyes of the eighty-year-old, the age of fifty is definitely young. I would say that you were born at the right time to reap the benefits of all these fantastic inventions. Explore your potential to the fullest in this ever-changing world, and you will certainly excel in everything you do.

Some of you might have heard of British author Sir Arthur Charles Clarke (1917-2008). He wrote many short stories and more than seventy books, both fiction and non-fiction. He was also an inventor and a futurist. You could very likely have come to know of Clarke because of the film *2001: A Space Odyssey*, based on his book of the same name. Many people found the film and the book fascinating and imaginative.

Clarke spearheaded the satellite communication systems in 1945; in 1994, he was nominated for the Nobel Prize, and in 1999, he was nominated for the Nobel Prize in literature. (Wikipedia 2008a) It is not an exaggeration to say that the world owes him thanks for the comfort of being able to communicate with one another via satellite and television. He was a visionary and half-a-century ahead of his time, even though the satellite communication has now surpassed Clarke's modest prediction in terms of its technology, size, and affordability.

The futuristic fantasy stories your grandparents read about during their childhood days have become a reality. In the 1980s, it was the decade of the microprocessor used in personal computers. In the 1990s, the decade of networks and communications emerged. It was symbolised by the World Wide Web, without which you and I could not connect to the world through Internet surfing. You should therefore change your mind-set and look at the world in a different perspective. Look from the sky just like a roc and widen your horizon. A paradigm shift is vital for you to excel in life and you need to constantly think outside the box. People who are left-brain-dominant are more logical than right-brain-dominant ones. When you dare to also think of the illogical, you are being creative and whole-brained. Bill Gates is a classic example.

Information is in the air and available at the touch of your computer keyboard. Search for knowledge through reading and surfing the Internet. If you are creative and read widely, you will foresee that microchips will soon be embedded into every facet of our life. In the hidden wiring within your walls, you may also find microchips that are able to detect any intruder. Your house furniture, bathroom, tables, and chairs may also have built-in chips. Instead of wasting time checking your medical history in case of emergency, the microchip in your clothing will provide all the data needed to save your life.

Probably within a decade or so, you may witness a three-dimensional universe in cyberspace, with virtual schools and universities. A virtual reality environment that joins people thousands of miles away may also come true one day. Our concern, however, is that if we rely too much on computers and robots, we may become ourselves robots with no feelings. Modern technology is a double-edged sword. It can make life easy as well as creating chaos for us. Nevertheless, you can rest assured that creative, right brain-dominant people will come out with inventions that may seem to be ridiculous and illogical.

When you are forward-looking and proactive, you can set goals which dovetail well with future trends in mind. You should realise that it is vital for you to master two or three languages and be computer-savvy to enable you to work with great efficiency. At the same time, you should also learn to enjoy and appreciate music, art, and sports; this will enable you to develop into a whole person who is innovative, who is intuitive, and who has good interpersonal skills to stand out distinctively among your peers.

It is inevitable that followers must dance to the tune of the leader. Therefore, make reading and lifelong learning habits so that you can always adapt to changes. One day, you can also be knowledgeable and a good Big Brother in your own right when others respect you, not for your tyranny but for what you have excelled in. As the old saying has it: nothing in life is certain except death and taxes. If you are visionary in your planning and equip yourself with knowledge and the dogged determination to succeed, you can surely excel in life.

When You Are an Avid Reader

As generations in the twenty-first century tend to grow up looking at digital images rather than words, reading is no more among the top priorities in life for many people. However, it will benefit you tremendously to know that if you do not read, you will be intellectually challenged because of the shallowness of your knowledge. Your horizon must therefore be so widened that you find it wise to allocate some of your precious time for reading. When you read, you are adding to your value by increasing your enormous wealth of knowledge and wisdom. Therefore, when you make reading your lifelong passion, your life will be further enriched.

If reading is to the mind what exercise is to the body, then reading will make you a thinker with vision. If each well-written book represents several years or decades of an author's experience, you will reap the vast benefits of a combined hundreds or even thousands of years of experience when you are an avid reader for life. You will not only nurture your language skills, you will also increase your critical thinking power. To be a high achiever, you need to be inspired by the successes of others. A time will also come when it is your turn to manifest your wisdom and experience to inspire others. You should therefore never stop reading, for as Confucius said, if you "stop reading for three days, your appearance will look disgusting."

Dr Theodor Seuss Geisel (1904-1991) of America was famous for creating rhymes, a talent nurtured by his mother, who sang to him before he slept. *The Cat in the Hat* became the definitive children's book. The author and illustrator wrote forty-four children's books, which have been translated into more than fifteen languages; over 200 million copies are held on dearly by children all over the world. (Tortus Technologies 2002-2004)

The beloved Dr Seuss was one of the prime movers in American literacy, starting from the mid-1950s. He wrote books that were part of the Beginner Books and Bright and Early Books series, which enabled young children to proudly declare, "I can read it all by myself." Dr Seuss was imagination personified for generations of children, and his distinctive legacy was in his 1975 book, *Oh, the Thinks You Can Think!* (Amazon. com, Inc. 2007)

This book has in abundance Dr Seuss's own wild imagination from the Guffs (fuzzy orange creatures with tails that have large furry balls) and the Snuvs (yellow creatures wearing colour-mismatched gloves), to the Bloogs (green, yellow, and blue creatures blowing by in the white sky above the black water), Zongs (with a tail that is fifteen times as long as the body and winds among the blue and pink mushrooms), the Rink-Rinker-Fink, and the Vipper of Vipp. Think of a race on a horse on a ball with a fish, and you are free to think creatively of the unthinkable in Jibboo. Colours and shapes in Dr Seuss's books were mismatched because almost all right-brain-dominant people think illogically.

If you dare to dream and think outside the box, like Dr Seuss, you are being visionary in your thinking. You are the leader, and those who are un creative and left-brain-dominant in their thinking wait for you to call the tune. The pioneers of powerful international brand names in all fields possess these traits of intuitiveness and innovativeness. They are an inspiration for your talent to be fully exploited. You too can inspire others in your own way other than excelling in your career: your integrity, forbearance, humility, optimistic outlook, kindness, and love for peace and not war. Read, reason, digest, and transfer whatever you have read and learnt into your practical life. Manifest positive values in your daily life.

Reach for the Sky is the best-selling story of Britain's most famous flyer, the courageous Sir Douglas Robert Steuart Bader (1910-1982), a hero of World War II. Authored by Paul Brickhill, the book was published in 1954 and was later made into a movie. Sir Douglas Bader was an inspirational British leader of the era and a legend, almost like a saint. He continued to fight despite having lost both legs in a pre-war flying accident. (Wikipedia 2008c)

Excelling in everything he did, the golden boy represented the Royal Air Force in acrobatics displays and was tipped to be in the England rugby team. However, all his dreams were shattered when he crashed his plane one afternoon in December while doing a particularly difficult aerobatic trick. Both his legs were amputated to save his life.

Sir Douglas Bader did not fly again until the outbreak of World War II, when his proven skill in the air convinced a desperate RAF to give him a squadron of his own. The rest of this story was just a collection of legendary incidents, such as when he was shot down in occupied France and his German captors were forced to confiscate his tin legs in order to stop him from fleeing. Bader faced his fate with the same charisma and determination that were to be an inspiration to those around him. When you read books of successful personalities, you will inevitably be moved by their visions and the inspiration imbued in them.

Malapropism

The Rivals (1775) was a comedy of five acts written by Richard Brinsley Sheridan (1751-1816), an Irish playwright. Sheridan's character Mrs Malaprop consistently used words and language malapropos, or inappropriately. When a word is wrongly used, it can cause embarrassment. Malapropism is therefore used to refer to a comical confusion of two similar-sounding words. One example is Mrs Malaprop's claim that she was the *pineapple* of politeness, when she meant the *pinnacle* of politeness.

In another instance, Mrs Malaprop wrongly expressed her fear when she said, "If I reprehend [should be *apprehend*] anything in this world, it is the use of my oracular [*vernacular*] tongue, and a nice derangement [*arrangement*] of epitaphs [*epithets*]!"

When you read to be a man of learning, you will not be putting yourself in the position of Mrs Malaprop. Your speech will not only be clear and precise, your choice of words will also be appropriate. In another aspect of your practical life, you should be sensitive to the fact that it is inappropriate to boast of your wealth to a bankrupt or your knowledge to an illiterate. The way you speak and the words you use reflect how self-restrained, empathetic, and learned you are.

Great Vessels Take Time to Build

If the recipients of Nobel Prizes are the benchmark, then we know that a great mind takes a long time to mature. Most laureates are of advanced age when they are honoured. They have overcome obstacles and failed experiments to be experts in their respective fields, to be reckoned with. As great oaks from little acorns grow, you must not be disheartened if you have failed or missed the boat at an earlier period of your life. Failures can be the motivating force for you to learn from your mistakes and rectify your weaknesses. Let bygones be bygones and never let an opportunity bypass you again.

You have to understand the implications of more haste, less speed. As Rome was not built in a day, you need time and patience to change and influence the people around you with your positive attitude. As long as you read, you can be a great vessel and a change agent to the society. I should say that being a source of positive inspiration for others to emulate is one of the best things you can be.

Great learning and great careers have all been thoroughly tempered through the test of time. Excellent literary works have to be repeatedly polished and revised and rewritten many times before they are finished. They must be steeled through the process of fine-tuning. Similarly, if you are serious and conscientious in learning, you will ultimately become a great learner and thinker. You will then be an authority in your chosen field. You must therefore be prepared to go through the waves and storms in life and be tempered in order to build up a great career of your own. While going through the process of learning, you will come to know that a man of great wisdom often appears slow-witted.

Arnold Joseph Toynbee (1889-1975), the British historian, took about thirty years to complete his twelve-volume analysis of the rise and fall of civilisations, *A Study of History,* which was published between 1934 and 1961. (*Encyclopedia Britannica* 2008) Edward Gibbon (1737-1794), the son of an English country gentleman, spent eleven years of his life, from 1776 to 1787, writing the six-volume series, *The Decline and Fall of the*

Roman Empire. (Biographies 2008) Gibbon was not merely one of the greatest historians of the world; he was also a great master of the English language.

When Sima Qian (145-85 BC) was castrated for incurring the wrath of Emperor Wu, he chose not to take his own life but to complete in jail his work, *The Records of the Grand Historian.* It contained 130 chapters of chronological Chinese dynastic histories; the book took eighteen years to complete. Another great Chinese historian, scholar, and statesman of the Song dynasty, Sima Guang (1019-1086), took sixteen years to finish his well-known work, *The Comprehensive Mirror as Mentor to Government.*

The Dream of the Red Chamber, one of the four great early Chinese novels, was first published in 1792. It was the work of Cao Xue Qin, who spent ten years reading through the draft and making a total of five amendments before it became an immortal masterpiece. The novel described the decline of an influential family and the ill-fated love stories between two young lovers.

Li Shizhen (1518-1593) was a great physician in the Ming dynasty of ancient China. Both his grandfather and father were also physicians. Though his father wanted him to be a government official, Li was not interested and failed the selection examinations three times. His first love was in reading medical books on herbs. Li dedicated thirty years of his life to compiling and verifying *The Great Compendium of Herbs*; he revised it three times and referred to more than 800 books while writing it. His masterpiece consisted of sixteen volumes and fifty-two chapters detailing the characteristics of nearly two thousand different herbs. He is an icon in Chinese herbs. (ClearHarmony Net 2001-2007)

The Russian novelist Leo Tolstoy (1828-1910) wrote *War and Peace,* which was first published from 1865 to 1869. It is well known that his wife, Sophie, copied out the long novel seven times from beginning to end, repeatedly making corrections until the work was flawless. (Bookyards.com 2005) You can now understand why this major masterpiece became one of the world's greatest novels. He strived for excellence regardless of the long period of time taken to achieve it. Can you imagine the tediousness of doing such editing work without the help of a computer?

You will have much to gain if you remember that a beautiful jade is cut and polished from an uncut jade stone, which is definitely not beautiful. In order to transform an uncut jade stone into a beautiful jade, there are many engineering processes involved. You are an uncut jade stone. You can also leave behind your own legacy if you have the will to do so. When you learn to reach out for your goals one step at a time and accumulate much experience, knowledge, and wisdom along the way, you will be a high achiever of your own standing one day.

Samuel Johnson (1709-1784), one of England's best known literary figures, was also an excellent lexicographer. He wrote *A Dictionary of the English Language* in ten years, between 1745 and 1755. He said, "Self-confidence is the first requisite to great undertakings." This quotation was not uttered for no reason.

Indeed, when Johnson was about to embark on his momentous dictionary, he went to see Lord Chesterfield, one of his patrons, for support but was made to wait for hours in vain. After the dictionary was finally published, the now eminent Johnson unexpectedly received a cheque from Chesterfield. Without a second thought, Johnson returned the cheque with his now famous "Letter to Chesterfield," dated 7 February 1755. (Wikipedia 2008e) In his letter Johnson reminded Lord Chesterfield of the humiliation he had suffered at the latter's office seven years ago.

"The notice which you have been pleased to take of my labours, had it been early, had been kind; but it has been delayed till I am indifferent, and cannot enjoy it; till I am solitary, and cannot impart it; till I am known, and do not want it," Johnson wrote satirically, with a strength of character.

Johnson had transformed his humiliation into strength and ultimately became a giant towering over Lord Chesterfield.

When You Have Self-Confidence

Self-confidence makes you a great vessel, albeit gradually. Excellent works are rare because you need time, perseverance, and self-confidence to achieve them. Shakespeare said, "Many strokes, though with a little axe, Hew down and fell the hardest-timber'd oak." (*Henry VI Part III*, act 2, scene 1) When you understand the philosophy behind this quotation, you are the water that wears the stone. A good seaman is known in bad weather; he is the one who can undergo severe tests. The powerful force of the wind will tell the strength of the grass. Through much perseverance and prolonged hard work, you can be like a blade of grass that manifests its hardiness in facing a gale. You will be the great vessel in the making.

At this juncture, let us ponder over the words of an unknown author in *Start with Yourself.* (Inspiration Peak 2007b) This man dreamt of changing the world when he was young but failed to do so. He then looked nearer and wanted to change only his country. This also turned out to be a wild goose chase. In his twilight years, he attempted to change only his family, thinking that they were the closest to him. He was again disappointed. Finally, while on his deathbed, he suddenly realised that if he had only changed himself first, then his family would have emulated him, followed by the change in his country and the world.

This wisdom is expressed in Confucianism, which stresses that a series of changes can only take place when you begin with self-cultivation or character building. With a paradigm shift in your thinking, you can then hope to put your house in order, administer your state well, and finally calm the country. Take small steps in the right direction, and you will have walked tens of thousands of miles in your lifetime, without making wrong choices.

When You Are Critical in Thinking

Ask yourself a series of questions using the 5Ws: What? Who? Which? When? And Where? Also ask yourself 1H: How?

Why do specialists command a higher premium for their services? The main reason is that they have excelled and are the authority in their professions. To reach that level, they have spent much of their precious time doing research and accumulating experiences in the course of their career. There is a great opportunity cost involved. Specialists are like great vessels which need a longer time to complete.

You may ask: What are my goals in life? Who can help me to achieve my goals? Which occupation suits me best? When can I achieve my plan? Where can I begin? How is my success plan going to work? Recall your relationship with the two most important persons in your life: yourself and your enemy. Remember the multiple intelligences that are in you and the success stories of great personalities, and choose the best option for yourself in your goal setting.

Do you go to work not knowing exactly what you are going to do for the day? Do you know what your plans are for the week, month, and year? If you do, then you know what you want to achieve in your career. If not, start reading books which interest you; go onto the Internet or ask around to find out more information before deciding on what you really want to be and do.

When You Know the Beauty of Simplicity

When you make your life simple, you will always have a smile on your face. You will have peace of mind, because you must be far from the madding crowd to think clearly and rationally. The reverse is also true. Life becomes complex when you use your limited time and energy to go for the unlimited wants, not knowing that this is like trying to catch the wind. You must realise early that at the end of your life cycle, you are actually returning to your starting point. You come to the world empty-handed, and that is the way you depart it. The philosophy here is that you must live your life: a fulfilling, happy, enriched and an enlightened one. This calls for you not to neglect the spiritual aspect of your life while toiling for the physical one.

In 1933, British author James Hilton wrote about a mystical, fictional, and harmonious society in his novel *Lost Horizon*. Since then, Shangri-La has become synonymous with a paradise on earth. The people living in Shangri-La were almost immortal and never grew old. Their life was simple. As a young boy in the 1950s, I saw the movie version of this book; the cinema depicted life in Shangri-La. In one scene, a beautiful young lady was carried out of Shangri-La on the back of her lover. While on the way out, the young lady suddenly changed into an old lady; she became short of breath. Her lover was so shocked to see the change that he lost his balance and fell. When he woke up, he was lying on a bed in a hospital. He then snuck out of the hospital to look for Shangri-La again, but it was not to be found anymore. I have remembered this film all my life.

The beauty of simplicity is that it is possible to epitomise the Shangri-La way of life, albeit in a different way. You need not have to feel old inwardly, though outwardly you are wasting away as years go by. You can be immortal in your thinking as long as you are full of zest in life. I shall discuss the steps to living a simple yet fulfilling life:

Be Simple in a Class of Your Own

Generally, class is a stylish quality in the form of clothes or social behaviour that attracts admiration. When you have class, elegance, style, or excellence are inherent in you. This class is not the privilege of the rich and powerful; it can also be manifested in the less privileged. I am talking about being sincere, humble, compassionate, and empathetic. For example, when your "yes" is "yes" and your "no" is "no," you have simplified matters. You do not have to argue with people, because you mean what you say; there is no need for others to weigh your words to see whether they are true or not, because they take you at your word. When you are polite, use edifying words, and season your speech with kindness, you are in a class of your own. Your class is of the intrinsic values and not in the monetary terms.

Once my wife and I went to a Mexican restaurant in town for lunch. While taking our orders, our waitress asked if we were retired teachers. When we replied in the positive, she told us that we spoke with gentleness. I immediately sensed that this waitress must have been spoken to rudely by some customers in the course of doing her duty. She reminded me of a similar instance years before, when a female shop assistant commended us when we were about to pay our bill; she appreciated the way we had conversed with her. You should always be courteous when you speak to others, regardless of their social standing. When you are simple and affable, you have class.

Be Simple in the Layout of Your Workplace

Fou Ts'ong (1934-present) is an international acclaimed pianist who won third prize in the International Frederick Chopin Piano Competition in Poland in 1995. This competition, first organised in Warsaw in 1927, is one of the oldest and most prestigious piano competitions in the world; it has been held every five years since 1955. It is known as the equivalent of the Nobel Prize in music. Fou Ts'ong attributed his success to his father Fu Lei, who was a disciplinarian. He said that his father was strict with matters concerning his own personal life; his father's writing desk was forever spotlessly clean, with everything neatly arranged. (Fu Min 2005: 89) When a person is disciplined, he does not waste his time looking for missing items. Have you ever counted the time you have wasted looking for misplaced books or stationery?

I once visited a secondary girls' school and was impressed when I entered the office of the headmistress. On her writing desk were only a pen and a file; the other documents and files were in their respective cabinets. No wonder she was deemed to be a high performing headmistress who was orderly in doing things. When your writing desk looks neat, clean, and void of piled-up files, you will not be pressurised unduly, thinking that a great amount of paperwork is awaiting your final touch. When things are neatly and properly placed, you will not waste time looking for items you need when you require them. Throw away unwanted items in your room, and make it simple and cosy for a pleasant working environment.

Be Simple in Your Answer

Generally, the great difference between the East and the West is that the former is implicit in their answers and the latter is explicit. People in the East find it rude to say "no"; they often make their life miserable because they have agreed to do something they do not want to do. However, their counterparts in the West are so blunt; they speak their minds and do not mince their words. A "no" is a "no," and it is loud and clear. If you do not want to be burdened unnecessarily with issues that you definitely cannot handle, just make it simple and say "no." In this way, you do not waste your time or the time of others.

If it is within your ability to say "yes," then go ahead and say so to offer your help. Since what you say is a promise that will be kept, you will be spared the hassle of having to convince others to believe in you.

In *The Emperor's New Clothes* by Hans Christian Andersen, a child who was naïve and could only see things as they were said that the emperor was naked. As the Chinese saying goes, "A word once spoken cannot be overtaken by a team of four horses"; what was said by the child could not be unsaid. Though his father was quick to reprimand him, the boy's remark was quickly echoed by the crowd. Though the child's mind was simple, he told the truth. The emperor was surrounded by sycophants who would never tell him the truth and made things complicated for many people.

Be Simple in Your Lifestyle

If you have studied economics, you should be familiar with the terms "needs" and "wants." A need is something you must have in order to survive. Your basic needs include food, shelter, and clothing. A want is something you desire to have. You may want to have a very expensive car to drive and live in a multimillion-dollar house, but those wants are not essential to your survival. You can drive a moderate car and live in a small house or apartment. Therefore, when you do not have too many wants in life, you have simplified your lifestyle, and that in itself is a blessing. You do not have to toil just to satisfy your wants or to keep up with the Joneses. There are many other things you can enjoy when you are simple in your lifestyle.

You are what you eat, so you should not over-eat. You should eat healthy food like vegetables and fruits, use less oil when cooking, and exercise regularly: playing games, jogging, or walking briskly. Those are the SEEDS of a simple lifestyle: Sleep well, Eat well, Exercise regularly, Drink a lot of water, and take

Supplements. Besides, you should also learn to appreciate music and art for their intrinsic value. As people are getting sick at a younger age nowadays because of a changing lifestyle, there is a necessity for you to live a healthy, simple, yet gracious lifestyle.

Summary

When you are not blinded by your negativity, you stand tall to view the scenery of a thousand miles. Helen Adams Keller's enthusiasm in living a life of enrichment, despite being deaf and blind, should serve as an inspiration to you. Orwell was almost flawless in his observation and visualisation in writing *Animal Farm* and *1984*. The quotation of "All animals are equal but some animals are more equal than others" is a gem. Orwell was almost prophetic in predicting that we would have to fight for our own freedom of speech and privacy in life. When the two novels are read together with Li's *The Study of the Thick Face and the Black Heart*, they become ever more relevant to our society of the twenty-first century. Orwell gives you an insight of what critical thinking and vision are. This also explains why some novels never become obsolete.

When you take a broad and long-term view in life, you are forward-looking; an avid reader and a man of learning who will not speak like Mrs Malaprop; a great vessel awaiting to take shape just as great oaks from little scorns grow; and critical in your thinking. You are to know the beauty of simplicity. James Hilton wrote in *Lost Horizon* about a mystical harmonious Shangri-La, which has become synonymous with a paradise on earth. Learn to be simple in a class of your own, in your workplace, answer, and lifestyle. You can live a simple yet a beautiful life when you look beyond your horizon.

Chapter Four

SMART Goals

Now that you have discovered the two most important people in your life, you can go on with your goal setting. When you know yourself and know your enemy, every battle will be a victorious one. You can set your goals with a purpose, because you know your strengths and the weaknesses which have prevented you from achieving progress all this while.

A Watched Pot Never Boils

Success is not the work of a single day; it is the progressive realisation of your dreams. When your goals are SMART, they are specific, measurable, attainable, realistic, and timely. A forty-year-old man who sets his goal to be a swimming champion is not being realistic, and his goal is not a smart one.

The age factor is an important point for you to consider when you set your goals.

There was a farmer who became anxious that his rice shoots were not growing as fast as they should. One day, he was inspired to go to his plot of land and pulled up every one of the young shoots in order to make them look taller. He returned home, fully satisfied with what he had done, and gleefully informed his family, "I have toiled the whole day, but I am excited that the rice shoots have all grown higher." His son gazed at his father in puzzlement before speeding to the field, only to find that all the young rice shoots had withered.

The moral of this story is that while we have ambitious goals, we must also have a down-to-earth style of working to achieve them. Always remember the old sayings "A watched pot never boils" and "More haste, less speed." Success is progressive and cannot be rushed.

There was another man who sold all his possessions and travelled to a faraway place, looking for a master to teach him the art of killing dragons. He spent three years learning the skill. When he returned to his hometown, people asked him what skill he had acquired. He then told them with great excitement that he had learned to kill dragons. When someone asked him, "Where can you find a dragon?" he was speechless. He had nowhere to apply the skill he had painstakingly learned. This man's goal was not smart because the dragons do not exist, and so he had no means of measuring his skill. His goal of killing dragons was not realistic.

Never Take Things for Granted

"The Necklace" is a short story by Guy de Maupassant (1850-1893), first published in 1884; it teaches a lesson about critical thinking. I remember this story very well because

I studied it during the first year of my university days in the 1970s. I would like to share this story with you.

Madame Mathilde Loisel was born with a very charming disposition, befitting a member of a noble family. As fate would have it, she married a junior clerk in the Ministry of Education, shattering all her dreams of belonging to upper-class society. She avoided seeing her rich old school friends because of her inferiority complex.

The chance of a lifetime came when she and her husband were invited by the Minister of Education to a dinner party. After learning of this invitation, she wept, not for joy, but in want of something presentable to wear. Her husband had saved 400 francs for a lark-shooting trip the following summer, but he gave her the money to purchase a new dress. Nevertheless, she was in low spirits for a few days because she had no jewellery to match her new dress. Her friend, Madame Forestier, was kind enough to lend Mathilde a superb diamond necklace.

Mathilde was the centre of attraction at the dinner party, and she was flattered. However, the glorious feeling did not last beyond the evening. Back at their apartment, Mathilde wanted to have one more look at her necklace before the mirror, but she uttered a cry because the necklace had gone missing. This discovery came as a thunderbolt to the couple. They searched everywhere for the necklace but failed to find it; they looked wretched all week.

They borrowed enough money to purchase a replacement. Mathilde and her husband were to live in abject poverty for the next ten years, working hard to repay this debt.

One Sunday, she saw Madame Forestier out walking; Mathilde was torn by conflicting thoughts but finally decided to greet her friend. She told Madame Forestier about losing the necklace, and her friend was deeply touched. However, she said, "Oh, my poor Mathilde! My necklace was imitation. It was worth at the very most 500 francs!"

From this story, we learn that Mathilde's goal was to make amends after showing off for an evening at the dinner party. People generally look at a person's outward appearance rather than their heart. Mathilde and her husband had had the wrong concept; they thought that their rich friend could not possibly have bought a fake diamond necklace; it looked real in the eyes of the poor. This was the greatest mistake of the couple: They assumed the necklace to be genuine.

Mathilde represents the poor, who do not see the hypocrisy of the rich, represented by Madame Forestier. She and her husband had a heart of gold when they took the responsibility upon themselves to replace the necklace. Mathilde paid a heavy price for her folly: plunging into poverty and drudgery that would take away her prized youth and beauty. Though she remained in the lower class of society, it was from this society that the real necklace was bought, through the help of real friends and family members.

Some readers dislike the story's implicit philosophical message that honesty is not the best policy. Nevertheless, it cannot be denied that while the world we live in may have people who are malevolent, there are also many kindhearted people who are like Mathilde and her husband. Discuss this story with your friends. What do you think would have happened if the husband and wife had not assumed that the borrowed diamond necklace was genuine?

The Fishermen

Aesop wrote many philosophical fables about fishermen. We shall look at this one concerning assumptions and expectations. Some fishermen cast their nets and were expecting a big catch. When the nets that were being pulled to the shore were heavy, they danced for joy in anticipation of a bountiful catch. However, when they dragged in the nets, they found but few fish; the nets were full of sand and stones. An old man said, "Let us stop lamenting; for sorrow is always the twin sister for joy. Just now you were overjoyed and should now have something to make you sad."

Back to the couple in "The Necklace"; wasn't it ironic that they had both joy and sorrow on that fateful occasion? What would have happened if they had asked and were told that the necklace was just a fake? Their greatest mistake was that they assumed.

In life you should not assume. I recommend the 2006 book *Never Say I Assume* by Tan Chin Nam with Larry Parr. Tan began as a Chinese trader and became a modern businessman, raconteur, and writer. The eighty-year-old Tan sums up his life experiences with the following statement: "Never say 'I assume,' because as a well-known saying goes, you make an 'Ass' out of 'U' and 'me.'" In setting your goals, it will benefit you not to take things for granted but substantiate your findings with facts and figures.

The Happiness of Fish

This witty story of two rival Chinese philosophers, recorded around the fourth century BC, is an absolute gem. The amusing conversation between Zhuangzi and Huizi tells us how people often make assumptions and look at things differently.

Zhuangzi and Huizi were strolling on Bridge Hao.

Zhuangzi: "The fish are swimming leisurely and happily in the water."

Huizi: "You are not a fish, how do you know that the fish are happy?"

Zhuangzi: "You are not me, how do you know that I don't know the fish are happy?"

Huizi: "I'm not you, so I certainly do not know what you know. You are definitely not a fish, and so you couldn't possibly know that the fish are happy."

Zhuangzi: "Please, let us go back to your original question. You ask me how I know the fish are happy, and this shows that you already know I know the fish are happy. I know it by standing on this bridge." (Ho 2009: 119)

This friendly intellectual argument tells us clearly that you are entitled to your opinion and others theirs. There is no need for you to echo the views of others if you do not agree with them. Therefore, when you set your goals, disregard the negative comments that may come to you. Stick to your goals.

A Collective Effort Is Powerful

In the current business world, networking is vital for success. You must be willing to co-operate with your friends and contacts. Integrity and good emotional intelligence are thus needed for the collective effort to be a worthwhile venture. The following argument between the mouth, the nose, the eyes, and the eyebrows, as to who should be on top of one another, was also recorded in ancient Chinese literature.

The mouth was having an argument with the nose on who should be on top. The mouth said, "I talk about history and current affairs; what makes you qualified to be on top of me?" The nose replied, "No one except me can distinguish the tastes of all food." The eyes told the nose, "I can differentiate very tiny and minute particles close at hand and observe things far away. Only I am qualified to be first in the listing." The eyes then said to the eyebrows, "What contributions have you got to be on top of me?" The eyebrows replied, "I might not be of practical use, but then I am like a distinguished guest in this world. What benefits can the guests bring to their host? If there are no guests at any function, then the protocol and the rituals have not been adhered to. Without eyebrows like me, what kind of appearance can you expect?" (Tangyulin 2008)

From this argument, we learn that the eyebrows were ignorant of their ability to keep sweat from the forehead from flowing into the eyes. Indeed, if a face has no eyebrows, it is not a face anymore. The eyebrows must be on top of the eyes and not below it, or else their function will be rendered useless. Hence, the four parts of the face should stop quarrelling and instead work together to play their roles and make the face look normal. The moral here is that in this world, no man is an island. You need to bear this in mind when you plan your goals. You need the co-operation of others to make your plans work.

Domains in Goal Setting

Your goal setting must therefore take into consideration the following domains:

1. Your character.

There is another old Chinese saying: "It is easy to defeat the bandits on the mountains but difficult to destroy the thief in your heart." You must therefore know your enemy and remove all the evil desires and negative attitudes from your heart and mind. Your first goal is to have integrity. When you have good character, your goals in life will be noble ones which benefit not only yourself but also the society you live in.

In character building, you must shun these four vices which can lead to a miserable life: wine, women, money, and temper. The wisdom here is that when you are drunk, you misbehave and act immorally. When you betray your spouse by becoming involved in an extra-marital affair, you bring shame to yourself and your family. When you are rich, especially if you amass wealth illegally, you are likely to be boastful, extravagant, demanding, and hot-tempered. A single slip in any of the four vices may cause you lasting sorrow. The error of a moment will become the regret of a lifetime. On the other hand, when you are a person of integrity and behave as a paragon of virtue, others will admire and emulate you.

When setting goals, it is inevitable that you will also take financial aspects into consideration. A man of noble character does need money but works for it honestly. You have to strike a balance between idealism and materialism. You may be an idealist who is for social justice or a believer in individualism. However, when you have cultivated your self, you will strike a balance between the two. You will try your best to achieve your goals, but not at the expense of others. There is humaneness in whatever you do; you will do unto others only what you want done unto you. You must also be a forgiving person, knowing that to err is human and to forgive is divine. When you are magnanimous enough to overlook the mistakes of others, others will come to respect you greatly.

Han Qi was a long-serving prime minister during the Song dynasty; he was well-known for being forgiving and enduring the mistakes of others. One night, Han Qi wanted to write a letter and asked a soldier to stand beside him and hold a candle for light. The soldier was indifferent after some time and the candle tilted, causing the hair of Han Qi to catch fire. The prime minister quickly put out the fire with his sleeves and calmly continued his letter writing. When he noticed that a different soldier was now holding the candle, he told the officer-in-charge not to punish the first soldier, saying that the latter had already learnt how to hold a candle. The qualities of compassion and forbearance touched the hearts of all his officers and soldiers.

On another occasion, Han Qi was hosting a feast for a high-ranking officer, during which two priceless jade cups were used to hold wine. During the feast, a servant accidentally knocked against the table, causing the two jade cups to fall to the floor, breaking into pieces. The servant was filled with such consternation that he placed his head on the ground, awaiting his punishment. Beyond everybody's expectation, Han Qi merely smiled and said to his guests that accidents did happen. The act of the servant was unintentional; he had done nothing wrong. (ClearHarmony Net 2001-2006)

If you believe that a forgiving heart never fails, you will overlook the mistakes of others. This quality will take you a long way forward in achieving your goals.

2. Your family.

Having a closely knit family should be your next goal. This requires you to spend quality time with your family members. Treat them with affection and respect. You may have elderly people, siblings, and young children at home; you should have compassion for them all and shower your love on them. Your tone in speaking and your body language must therefore be like the forms of water, fitting in well with all the members of the family. The family members are the closest to you; they share your happiness, concerns, and sorrows. Hence, when you set your goals in life, put aside time to share them with your family. When you put your house in order, you will then have a comfortable home to return to after a hectic day outside.

You may know the song "Home Sweet Home." It comes from an anonymous Sicilian air, with lyrics written in 1822 by John Howard Payne (1791-1852), an American actor and playwright. It was first sung in Covent Garden, England, in 1823 as part of the opera *Clari, the Maid of Milan.* Two out of the five stanzas of the lyrics are quoted here:

Home, Sweet Home

Mid pleasures and palaces though we may roam,
Be it ever so humble, there's no place like home;
A charm from the sky seems to hallow us there,
Which, seek through the world, is ne'er met with elsewhere.
Home, home, sweet, sweet home!
There's no place like home, oh, there's no place like home!
To thee I'll return, overburdened with care;
The heart's dearest solace will smile on me there;
No more from that cottage again will I roam;
Be it ever so humble, there's no place like home.
Home, home, sweet, sweet, home!
There's no place like home, oh, there's no place like home!
(PoemHunter.com 2007)

Your home is your refuge. Shower the members of your family with love at every opportunity, and you will never regret this when you grow old.

3. Your spiritual life.

If you are an atheist, you may think that the idea of God is meaningless. Your values and beliefs may even differ from other free thinkers. It is said that happiness is the ultimate value that atheists stand for. You may then have to relate this part of the discussion confining to your own values.

This is an important domain, because if you are too materialistic, you show no fear of God. You will be tempted to do things against the law. For example, you may have amassed a fortune through illegal transactions or dealings that are detrimental to society, or you may have stabbed someone in the back to get a promotion. This is going against the grain of making an honest living. If you are an unethical professional, then you are at most literate but not educated.

Your spiritual nature is manifested when you fear God the creator. Always make it your goal in life to live happily from day to day, without your conscience being pricked. You will be able to sleep soundly without waking in the night because you dream that your foes are after you. When you balance your physical life and spiritual life, you will live harmoniously. You are a letter of recommendation when the virtues of integrity are manifested in your speech and deeds.

Confucius was a great philosopher, humanist, scholar, and political analyst. He taught, without prejudice, students of different socio-economic backgrounds. He had three thousand students under his tutelage; seventy-two of these sages went round China spreading humanistic thinking on the harmony between humans and nature, between humans and society, between people, and between one's mind and body.

The conflicts between and within nations, the destruction of the environment, and the drive to control the world's natural resources are the result of a lack of harmony. The world has indeed not been kind to God's creation. In 1988, seventy-five Nobel Laureates met in Paris and published this resolution: "If mankind were to continue to survive in the twenty-first century, they must go back 2,500 years to absorb the quintessence of the wisdom of Confucius." (AoCM 2002: 40)

Hence, if you take time off to meditate, you will learn that material comfort is not the only important thing in life. Our folly is that we assume we will live to a ripe old age, when in actual fact we do not even know what will happen tomorrow. You must therefore always remember your creator; do not only think of storing up wealth for yourself. When you balance your life, you will live to enjoy the fruit of good planning until the twilight of your life.

4. Your circle of friends.

When you grow old, you must have three things to accompany you to spend your remaining years in happiness: an old spouse, old friends, and old savings. You need to have your spouse, who understands you through and through; old friends, who can talk about the good old days; and enough money to see you through the old age. When you live at home, you rely on your parents; when you live outside the house, you depend on your friends. When you have no friends to confide in or for networking in your business, you are doing things alone. Without friends, your life will be a very lonely and an unhappy one.

In ancient China, the four most joyous occasions were having a welcome downpour after a long drought, running into an old friend in a distant land, enjoying a wedding feast, and seeing one's name in the examination passing list. The second joyous occasion implies that friends are important to you in your life. It is vital that you take the initiative to be friendly, proactive, and trustworthy. Are you sociable, or are you a wet blanket who prevents your friends from enjoying themselves? People are gregarious, so a life without friends to talk to, to share our sorrows, and to laugh heartily with is a meaningless one. Do you fondly remember your old friends, classmates, college mates, colleagues, or close relatives? Send them an email, text them a message, or give them a call; you may be surprised at how grateful they are that you remembered them.

The Sky Is the Limit (1943) is obviously a sweet reminder of an enjoyable trip back in history to many senior citizens. The movie was made during the height of World War II to appeal to a war-time fan base. There were a few musical numbers and outstanding dance routines which could make you roar with laughter throughout film.

I mention this movie because I did not know that it existed. A good friend in Germany told me about this movie after seeing it on TV. He knew I was writing this book, and so he emailed me about the movie. This goes to show that the more friends you have, the more information you can get in this digital world. Thus, you must be sociable and not be a Lone Ranger. You do need friends to enrich your life.

If you read about the harrowing aftermath of the tsunami that devastated many countries in December 2004, you might have heard the story of a highly unlikely friendship between a baby hippo named Owen and a 130-year-old giant tortoise named Mzee (Mm-Zay). Isabella Hatkoff and Craig Hatkoff wrote two picture books about the pair—*Owen & Mzee: The True Story of a Remarkable Friendship* and *Owen & Mzee: Language of Friendship* (the latter co-written with Paula Kahumbu)—that touched the hearts of children all over the world. (NPR 2008)

Owen was rescued by villagers in Kenya after being stranded following the tsunami. To the surprise of everyone, the orphan hippo looked to the elderly tortoise for refuge. They developed a genuine bond with each other and became inseparable friends in adversity. They were to be seen swimming, eating, and playing together. Visitors witnessed this incredible spectacle first hand at Haller Park, which was open every day to the public. Owen was eventually moved to a bigger pond at the park so that he could socialise with other hippos. The differences between Owen and Mzee were not a hindrance to a lasting friendship. They have shown us that all men are brothers.

"Auld Lang Syne" is a famous song from the old Scots dialect. It is a traditional Scottish song written by Robert Burns (1759-1796); the title means "days gone by" or "long ago." The song is often sung at the end of a farewell gathering or an anniversary dinner for old boys and girls. Do you know the song? If not, here are the lyrics:

Should auld acquaintance be forgot,
And never brought to mind?
Should auld acquaintance be forgot,
And auld lang syne?

Chorus:

For auld lang syne, my dear,
For auld lang syne.
We'll take a cup o' kindness yet,
For auld lang syne.

5. Your financial planning.

A person who gets richer through corruption becomes poorer in integrity. Riches obtained through unrighteous means are nothing but floating clouds to you. Thus, you must only accept wealth and rank earned through proper channels. It is not wrong to desire for money; it is wrong when the wealth gained is ill-gotten money. To the corrupt, Confucius asked, "Do you feel at ease?"

In order not to fall into the temptation of asking for bribes, thereby making a shipwreck of your conscience, you ought to set your financial goal with the proper perspective. You have to learn to be very frugal with your money, and frugal habits start when we are young. When you get your first pay, you should immediately start implementing your financial plan. Consult your parents, friends, or a financial planner for advice. Learn how to manage your finances prudently so that you will not always be in debt. Indeed, if you force yourself to start saving after getting your first pay, you will enjoy your retirement without having to live like a pauper. Save for a rainy day.

In your financial planning, you have to make a clear distinction between needs and wants. In economic terms, a need is something you must have, like food; you need to eat in order to survive. A want is something you would like to have, but it is not absolutely necessary. Nevertheless, if you can have it, you will feel good. You may want to have a big car, but it is not a need. It is not necessary for you to own a big car to survive, because you can drive a smaller car or use mass transit.

The next question you may ask is whether you want to travel now and pay later, or save enough money first before you travel. Are you going to pay a high interest for your credit card overdraft, or are you going to settle the bills every month? My advice to you is not to spend your future money in advance. As far as possible, do not keep up with the Joneses by spending unnecessarily. You will be happier living within your means and investing your savings wisely.

An elderly man was having lunch with a group of young men. One of them asked, "What is the best car to drive?" Names of expensive, prestigious, and trendy brands were mentioned by the young men. The elderly man then told them, "The best car to drive is one that has been paid for." The same is true as to the best house to buy. The wisdom of the elderly man is that when you do not have any debt, you have financial freedom. This should be your ultimate aim in setting your financial goals.

You have to prepare for a rainy day, like paying for emergency medical fees or helping family members who need financial help. When your financial goal is properly planned, you will have fewer problems with your loved ones and friends. It may help to remind you that of all types of anger, the anger of being poor and in debt was the most difficult one to contain. Never provoke a poor person to anger, because out of frustration of being in want of money, they may turn very fierce and physical.

It is advisable for you to stay away from credit cards. Even though you have to use them, do so as their master and not their slave. When your debt snowballs to an amount beyond redemption, life will become miserable. Thus, you must be disciplined in using your credit cards. Indeed, if you need to raise money to pay for a huge credit card balance, you may fall into the temptation of accepting bribes. That is the beginning of deviating from one's principles in life.

On 12 December 2006, I watched an interview on CNBC with Warren Buffett, the second richest man in the world, who had donated $31 billion to charity. He advised young people to stay away from credit cards and invest in themselves. He said that money does not create humans, it was humans who created money. You are to live your life as simple as you are and do what makes you feel good. You need not wear brand names; just wear clothing that feels comfortable. You should not waste your money on things you do not really need. Always invest for the long term; just live happily and give others no chance to rule your life. You are also encouraged to bear in mind that "No one can make you feel inferior without your permission; remember, they are no better." (Robin Bal 2006-2007)

6. Your health.

This is another very important aspect in your goal setting. Without health, there will be no wealth. Ironically, many people tend to sacrifice their health when they are young to accumulate more wealth, only to spend that wealth on treatment when they are old. You have to face the reality that health is too important and valuable for you to neglect. When you lose your wealth, you can still work to earn it back. However, when you lose your health, your family members and loved ones suffer with you. In your goal setting, you must therefore resolve to maintain your health by choice and not by chance.

Your health enemies include chronic degenerative diseases like heart disease, cancer, diabetes, obesity, Alzheimer's, osteoporosis, arthritis, and skin diseases. In order not to be a victim, you need to exercise and take in nutritional supplements. We can only control our life by taking initiatives to keep us healthy; we cannot control pollution in the air, water, or sea; we cannot control noise pollution; vegetables and fruit are often sprayed with pesticides, milk is often contaminated, and meat often contains anti-biotics. Hence, you must also inculcate the habit of drinking good water, sleeping well, and eating fresh fruits and vegetables. Have more wellness but less medicine.

A pupil was struggling to write an essay about the seven wonders of the world; her teacher told the class what she thought the seven wonders were: to see, to hear, to touch, to taste, to feel, to laugh, and to love. We often take life for granted, so much that we forget to be grateful for what we have. The teacher taught a simple yet very profound lesson: always count your blessings.

Besides being healthy physically, you should make sure you are emotionally healthy too. Involve yourself in activities like music, art, and sports to help release your tension. You may be familiar with the saying, "All work and no play makes Jack a dull boy." So learn how to have a life of enrichment; do not merely live. This should be one of your goals in life. As laughter is the best medicine for a healthy body and mind, you will want to have friends who make you laugh heartily to brighten your days. Keep cheerful friends, for they are optimistic, and learn from them.

7. Your career.

A job is different from a career. A job is a position in which you are currently gainfully employed; it is what you are doing today. It is unlikely that you will keep your first job until your retirement, because most workers change jobs many times in their working lifetime. When you treat your job as a job, you are likely to be a clock-watcher, not willing to remain in office any longer than necessary.

A career is your chosen profession or an occupation you love and enjoy doing. When your job becomes your career, you will dedicate your time and effort in doing it. You will walk the extra mile in your dream career; the monetary reward is of secondary importance. Self-actualisation is your ultimate goal in life, and you want to leave a legacy in your chosen field. You can stand out distinctively in your chosen career if you put your heart, mind, and soul into it.

In making your career a success, try to explore ways in which you can make your work more productive and satisfying. If you spend time tracking work processes, you will be able to identify unproductive components. Improve them or delegate them to keep from being overloaded with trivial duties. You should consider changing jobs if you find the current one not suitable. As a rolling stone gathers no moss, you ought to decide what you want to be in life and stick to your decision but change jobs if it is unsuitable.

Your goals should not be achieved unscrupulously but through hard work and determination. When you plant melons you will get melons; sow beans and you will get beans. As you sow, so will you reap. Your goals must therefore be legitimate and worthwhile. Avoid the negative attitude of having to "rob Peter to pay Paul" to achieve your goals because it manifests your weakness in character and a lack of self-confidence. You need to achieve your goals progressively: to travel a long distance, you have to take the first step; to climb a high mountain, you must begin from the lowest point.

During the Jin dynasty (AD 265-420) in ancient China, there was a much-respected general by the name of Tao Kan, who was an orphan from a poor family. His mother was very strict with him and wanted him to grow up to be a man of integrity. As an officer, Tao Kan was responsible for the fish ponds of a county, and he took home some salted fish. His mother disapproved of these petty gains and chastised her son in a letter, telling him to learn to be honest in his work:

As an officer in the county you ought to be honest and upright in your work. How could you have exploited your power by giving me things belonging to the government? They might not be silver and gold or anything that was expensive but just a few fishes, but this action of yours goes against the conscience of a person and is not right. I am not happy at all but feel sad and worried for you. You must not deviate from your conscience for some petty gains.

The letter touched the heart of Tao Kan, who then repented of his act and quickly wrote back to his mother, assuring her that he would not repeat the mistake. (Jiangxi 2006)

In comparison, we can say that taking a few fishes from the county was nothing compared to the act of some high-ranking officials who embezzle public funds. You must therefore always remember that your goals should be achieved through honest and noble ways. Goals well set and closely monitored are work well done. You must do your work with no ulterior motives.

8) Your marriage.

This aspect may not be relevant if you have decided, for one reason or another, to remain single. However, it may help to enlighten you on the other side of the story if you read on.

In the ancient societies, married children lived with one of the spouse's parents in the same housing compound, and the extended family was very closely knit. The couple could count on the help of the old and young at home for physical, emotional, and financial support. The opposite is true for modern parents living in the city. Young parents nowadays work, and they are often forced to employ complete strangers to care for their children (unless the grandparents are staying with them).

When couples fail to fulfil their roles as caring parents because they are too busy pursuing their careers, problems are the result, especially if they do not spend quality time with their children. These children in turn cause disciplinary problems in their schools. The negative chain effect continues when they drop out of schools and become a menace to society. As such, you should seek advice from well-meaning elders who can offer you help.

Beauty is skin deep, and romantic love is at best a superficial feeling, so you should choose your life partner based on good character to avoid unnecessary arguments and conflicts that can put a stress in your married life. A healthy marriage will reduce economic stress and strain by sharing costs; it also widens the support network from family members and friends and improves the health of the couple when their bad habits are discarded for the love of each other.

A prudent wife or an understanding husband will be instrumental in achieving your goals. You should continue to respect your parents and parents-in-law after your marriage. A wise and global-travelled lady, ninety-three years old, once told me to ponder over a well-known saying, "A daughter is a daughter for all of your life; a son is a son until he gets a wife." Only you will know whether this applies to you or not.

Here is an anecdote for you:

The human resource manager of a big firm called a hundred of his married male staff for an assembly. He asked those who were afraid of their wives to stand on his right and those who were not afraid of their wives to stand on his left. Ninety-seven men moved to the right, and one moved to the left. The manager asked the two standing in the middle to explain why they did not move to the right or left.

One man said, "My wife always tells me to take the middle path." The other answered, "I tried to call my wife on her i-Phone but failed. She always tells me to consult her before making any decision."

The ninety-seven men on the right were full of admiration for the one on the left, but not for long. The lone ranger said, "My wife always warns me not to go to a crowded place."

Having a happy family is one of the joys of life. This calls for respect for one another in a family. When both husband and wife exercise forbearance, and not dominion over each other, a house becomes a home.

Be a Doer of Your Plan

A well-thought-out plan must have a deadline for its completion. By following through your plan conscientiously, day after day, you are bound to succeed. As you have already seen, the beginning is always the most difficult. This is the same when it comes to writing your plans. You must remember that when you fail to plan, you plan to fail. Every minute of your time must be spent wisely and accounted for.

Develop daily, weekly, monthly, and yearly plans for you to monitor the progress. Make sure your plans are SMART: specific, measurable, attainable, realistic, and timely. As you have only twenty-four hours a day, you must make full use of every minute. Follow your plan closely so that your time is spent wisely. Here are some pointers for you to be a doer of your plan:

Always Have Good Mental Notes

There was a painter in the Song dynasty who was excellent at painting pictures of bamboo. As he had planted many bamboos around his house compound, he was able to notice the changes of the plant's shapes and colours at the turn of each of the four seasons. He could thus easily visualise the images of bamboo to make his paintings look real. Many people came and asked him to paint pictures of bamboo because of his talent in drawing. His good friend who was a poet wrote about his paintings and said that "when he paints, he has the pictures of bamboo in his mind." The painter was extremely self-confident and knew the plant's details by heart.

Therefore, when you are a doer of your plan, you must have already known exactly what you want and what you are going to do, as if the pictures of bamboo are already in your mind. You take each step of your plans with full confidence and accuracy. This calls for consistency in adhering to your plans and monitoring activities. However, you should modify your plans to suit the changes of time if you have to.

Liezi wrote a story about a monkey trainer in the state of Song, who had with him a large group of monkeys. After having been with the monkeys for a long time, he came to know their temperament through and through. Similarly, the monkeys also began to understand the language of their master.

The trainer always shared his family's food with the monkeys. Then came a difficult time when there was a shortage of food; the ration for each monkey was cut from eight chestnuts a day to seven. In order not to displease the monkeys, the trainer deliberately tested them by saying, "I shall give you three chestnuts in the morning and four in the evening. Would that be enough for you?" The monkeys bared their teeth to show their displeasure for the poor deal.

The trainer wittily replied, "Since you consider that deal unfair, I shall now give you a better offer. How about giving you four chestnuts in the morning and three in the evening?" On hearing these words, the monkeys were overjoyed. They all prostrated on the ground and wagged their tails to thank their master for his generosity. (Huaxia 2000)

This story originally referred to someone who plays fast and loose, who behaves insincerely or unreliably. It now means someone who is inconsistent. Good governance has consistent policies which do not change immediately after they have been implemented. Likewise, your goal setting and planning must also be consistent once you have decided upon them. The pictures of bamboos must remain crystal clear in your mind.

Be Disciplined

When you stop at a red traffic light, and it is after midnight, do you wait for the light to turn green before proceeding? If you wait for the light to turn green, even though there are no other cars, then your passengers will know you are a well-disciplined person who can be trusted to work independently on your own.

A Chinese idiom, "Giving three orders and five injunctions" (*san ling wu shen*), means that orders must be repeated several times before people understand. The words "three" and "five" also mean "many times" in the Chinese language.

During the Spring and Autumn period (770-476 BC), Sunzi presented his book on *The Art of War* to the king of Wu. The king was very interested in the book and asked Sunzi, "Can a detachment of women soldiers be trained?" Sunzi replied, "Yes." The king then selected 180 court ladies to be instructed by Sunzi, who divided the court ladies into two groups. Two group captains were then selected from among the king's beloved concubines.

When the troops had lined up, Sunzi gave them detailed instructions pertaining to the requirements and methods of training. He repeatedly cautioned them to be disciplined and to strictly follow orders. When the court ladies said that they had all understood what was to be done, Sunzi placed many weapons on the ground. This was to warn the ladies that discipline must be maintained at all time and any indiscipline would not be tolerated.

Sunzi then gave a command to the ladies: "Right turn!" Instead of following the order, all the court ladies burst into laughter. Sunzi said, "The commands have not been clearly explained to you; this is my fault as an instructor." He then repeated his explanation to them.

This time a new command was given. When Sunzi shouted his order, "Left turn!" the ladies still did not follow the command; instead, they continued to laugh. Sunzi said, "All instructions have been made clear to you. Now that you have not obeyed the orders, the captains are at fault." He then ordered that the two captains be executed.

When the king of Wu heard about this, he hurriedly sent someone to plead with Sunzi for lenience. However, the request was not granted. Sunzi said, "Since I have accepted the order to be the instructor, I have to act according to military discipline." The two group captains were then beheaded. Another two new captains were then chosen to fill the vacancies.

After that, the court ladies did not dare disobey orders, and they went through the military drilling without a hitch. The king of Wu was so impressed by Sunzi's ways of enforcing discipline that he appointed him chief general. (Baidu 2008a)

The lesson we can learn here is that when you discipline yourself, you can get things done successfully. When the whole organisation is disciplined like you, the organisation will grow.

Be Resourceful

You can successfully execute your plans when you are resourceful. There will always be obstacles blocking your path of life, and you need resourcefulness to come up with more solutions to your problems. For example, how do you deal with the unexpected? To be resourceful, you need to read widely and humbly ask for advice from whoever will help you. Do invest your time and money in reading books and attending conferences, seminars, and enrichment courses to widen your knowledge and network.

If more fishes are to be caught, you need to go to the blue ocean with a bigger and stronger fishing net. Similarly, if you want more ideas and connections, you have to spread your horizon by meeting more people. Their stories of success and failure will be an eye-opener to you. As every failure is a valuable lesson learnt, you should not fear it but go ahead with your plan; you must have the self-confidence to execute it as scheduled. When you are resourceful, you are also good at acting according to circumstances.

King Zhao of the Warring States period (475-221 BC) in China was desperately looking for top brains to help him administer his state. One of his ministers, Guo Wei, told him this story:

"Once there was a king who offered hundreds of ounces of gold for a horse which could run 500 miles a day. The man he sent out came back with a pile of bones of a dead steed for half the gold. The king was outraged that even dried bones cost that much. The man said, 'When people come to know that you would pay so much for a dead horse, they will surely try their very best to get you a good steed for a handsome reward.' True enough, the king soon received three winged steeds within a year. If you are serious in getting top talents to serve you, why don't you start me off and treat me as a dead horse so that other people of high calibre will flock to you?"

After hearing the story, King Zhao realised that Guo Wei was a wise man. He then recognised the worth of his minister, respected him as a teacher, and rewarded him abundantly to show that capable leaders should be given their due respect. Within a couple of years, great talents from different states went to help King Zhao and made his state more powerful.

You can learn from the resourcefulness of Guo Wei in adapting himself to changing conditions. He presented his case with considerable subtlety.

Be as Wise as Water

You must be able to adapt yourself to the environment surrounding you so that your goals can be achieved. Water does not have a definite form; it can reshape itself to suit its environment. It can come in the forms of vapour, dew, ice, and rain without changing its characteristics. The rain comes down in drops which form rivers before flowing into the ocean. Water flows from a high ground to a low one and finds its direction and equilibrium; is a great equaliser because all men, rich and poor, must drink water to quench their thirst. It is a source of life, for without water, all living things will die. The power of water is also manifested when there is a flood. Nothing can stop the water from showing its strength.

When you possess the wisdom of water in your goal setting, you will be able to plan to nurture yourself into someone with integrity and wisdom. Your friends will come to you for advice. They will also come to share with you their happiness and sorrow, because you are good in your interpersonal skill. There is nothing in this world that can stop you from achieving your goals when you are as wise and flexible as the water. You will be able to overcome all obstacles because you are firm but gentle like water. Drops of water can ultimately pierce a hole through a hard rock, just like soft worms can penetrate hard wood. Similarly, a copper a day makes a thousand coppers in a thousand days, and a hemp rope is able to ultimately saw through wood. How could that happen? Perseverance is the word. With it, even little strokes can fell great oaks. What you need to do is to be firm and tenacious from within your heart, not just superficially.

Your Byword

Synonyms of "byword" include slogan, reproach, and proverb. A byword is a common saying or something well known for a specific characteristic. It can also be an object of scorn or interest. Generally, a byword is a person famous for being infamous. For example, a wicked person's name is a byword for cruelty, and the crime of a notorious robber can make him a byword. Similarly, if your town has a spate of break-ins, you can say that the town has now become a byword for robbery.

As "byword" can also refer to a person or an object of interest, I would say that the name of a righteous person can be a byword for kindness and integrity. If you are a person of good character, your name can also be a byword for excellence, diligence, compassion, generosity, and friendliness. As for an object, sometimes we tend to use a byword to compare different brands of products. For example, in the phrase "Bosch is the Rolls-Royce of all power tools," Rolls-Royce is the byword because we associate the name with excellent cars.

In your circle of friends, you may attach to each of them a byword in which you form an opinion on their character. When the group talks about people always being late for appointments, names of those who are habitual late-comers will be mentioned. Generally, you tend to remember well the names of those who stand out distinctively in their character. How would you like to be remembered by your friends? Would you like to become a byword as a respectable and likable person? You stand to be counted when you are a paragon of admirable character.

You Are What You Want to Be

"The Story of the Pencil" comes from Paulo Coelho's popular book *Like the Flowing River*. In this story, a grandmother stops writing her letter to tell her grandson not to look at the pencil she was holding as just an ordinary pencil. She told him to possess the qualities of a pencil: the ability to do great things, with God's guidance; the ability to go through the ordeal of being sharpened to remain sharp; and the ability of an eraser to rub out any mistakes. She added, "What really matters in a pencil is not its wooden exterior, but the graphite inside." This implies that you must guide your heart; and it always leaves a mark. (Wordpress.com 2008)

You are what you want to be, and no other person can live your life for you. When you understand that your life is what you make it out to be, you become focused on planning for your future. It does not matter how others look at you, because no two individuals are alike. You then decide what your goals are and how you are going to achieve them. You must be able to think independently and stand by what you say. Learn from the pencil.

Emulate Successful People

Confucius was a great thinker, philosopher, and educator who loved orchids because he found emotional sustenance in them. In Book Six, Volume Four of *The Family Talks of Confucius,* there was a record of his praising the orchid. He said, "To stay together with a kindhearted and charitable person is like going into a room full of orchids. After you have been in the room for some time, the fragrance of the orchid is not apparent anymore because you have already been transformed to become part of the fragrance. To stay with an evil and wicked person is like staying in a fish market. After you have been in the place for some time, the offensive smell is no more apparent because you have also been transformed into part of the stink. As there is red being hidden in crimson and so is there black being concealed in pitch-dark. Hence a gentleman must be careful of the character of those who stay together with him." (Baidu 2013b)

You can benefit from associating with people of noble character, whereas a long exposure to a bad environment and influence accustoms you to evil ways. Confucius also said that if you do not know the son, look at his father; if you do not know a person, look at his friends; if you do not know the supreme ruler, look at his envoy; if you do not know the land, look at its bushes and trees. Thus, when you stay near vermilion, you get stained red, and when you stay near ink, you get stained black. Therefore, you ought to follow successful people who have integrity, those who are positive and proactive. Emulate them and you will look beyond your horizon to be a high achiever.

Summary

Set goals that are SMART: sustainable, measurable, achievable, realistic, and timely. Learn from the farmer who pulled up every one of the young shoots to make them look higher, only to find them withered; the saying, "A watched pot never boils," warns us against giving in to impatience. You should also not take things for granted; "The Necklace," "The Fishermen," and "The Happiness of Fish" are good testimonies to this. The argument about who is the greatest among the mouth, nose, eyes, and eyebrows reflects the ignorance of the organs, which do not know the power of teamwork.

You have also been guided as to the domains in your goal setting. You need to nurture your character; spend quality time with your family; ponder over your spiritual life and avoid indulging in the pursuit of worldly treasures; have a circle of bosom friends who can be with you in times of both happiness and sorrow; spare no effort in executing your financial plans; live a healthy life by choice and not by chance; treat your job as your career and be an expert in your own field; and make your marriage work.

As a doer of your plan, you are expected to be fully prepared before embarking on it. It always helps to have the mental notes with you so that you know exactly what to do. When you are disciplined, you do not disobey orders, as shown in the story of "Giving three orders and five injunctions." In executing your plan, resourcefulness is called for, and you are to be as wise as water to be flexible in implementing your plan. Your byword can be in the positive sense, and you are what you want to be. Learn from successful people to improve on your SMART goals.

Chapter Five

Understanding the Thirty-Six Stratagems (Part I)

A stratagem is a plan or trick, especially to deceive the enemy. The Greeks used the stratagem of the wooden horse to capture Troy. In ancient China, there are thirty-six stratagems in the art of war; they are especially important when maneuvering an army into a favourable position. The stratagems were first recorded in the official history of Southern Qi about 1,500 years ago; they were published in 1941 in Chengdu, Sichuan Province. They were later compiled into a book called *The Secret Art of War: The 36 Stratagems*. (Henic Lund 2007)

The thirty-six stratagems are grouped into six sets; the first three are meant for application when one has the advantage over others; the other three are for when one is at a disadvantage. In warfare, you need to be able to read the next move of your enemy in order to win the battle. Those who use the thirty-six stratagems effectively will have a slight edge over their opponent; these stratagems, then, are a necessary means to an end.

However, the stratagems have their negative aspects. They are now being employed in marketing to plan crafty tricks which are abhorrent to honest businessmen. You may find some of your friends, business associates, or opponents making use of the thirty-six stratagems to achieve their ulterior motives. As such, the stratagems can be viewed as a double-edged sword. They are vital and necessary in times of war, but some unscrupulous people may use them unethically in business and social circles.

Some people do not call a spade a spade. It is therefore advisable for you to know about these stratagems so that you will not fall into their snares. Nevertheless, if you are compelled to apply any of the thirty-six stratagems in life, you should weigh the pros and cons of the stratagem you are going to employ. Will you make a shipwreck of your integrity? Are you going to trick your friends? Can you modify the stratagem, if you have to use it, to remove the unpleasant insinuations that you might not be honest? Will you use them when you have to turn ill luck into good? What if your life is in peril and you have to protect yourself? You may not want to have anything to do with the first thirty-five stratagems, but you may make use of the last stratagem, which is to run for your life.

Thus, the knowledge of these stratagems will help you tremendously in dealing with people of complex character; it will also prepare you to be on the alert of imminent danger. You have to look beyond your horizon and not to take people at face value; learn to disregard their appearance. Remember that there are people whose faces are thicker than the wall of a fort; they are so thick as to become formless, and their hearts are so black that they become colourless because their wickedness is veneered by their hypocrisy.

Stratagems to be used when one has a slight edge over others

Winning Stratagems

Stratagem No. 1: Cross the sea under camouflage (*man tian guo hai*, 瞒天过海)

An emperor was leading a troop of 300,000 soldiers to a battle when they were obstructed by the sea. Fearing that the emperor would not cross the sea to fight the battle, the army's general quickly thought of a plan; he enclosed a barge with a very colourful tent and ushered the emperor inside. All civil and military officials were ordered to make merry by drinking and singing so that the emperor could be free from all anxieties. In the midst of their enjoyment, the emperor suddenly heard the sound of roaring waves. Curious, the emperor lifted up the curtain of the tent and saw that he and the 300,000 soldiers were almost to the other side of the rolling sea. The general's crossing the sea by a trick was a deceptive tactic. The emperor was so used to the sight of colourful tents that he did not expect anything unusual to happen. His general then created the impression of familiarity and crossed the sea with a trick.

When you are familiar with something, you tend to take it for granted. A strategist will take advantage of this and maneuver the unseen. Therefore, you must always think carefully before making decisions.

In practical life, a marketing team met to discuss how to increase the sales of a bottled spice product. Every executive was trying to come up with an innovative and down-to-earth solution. Someone suggested enlarging the size of the hole in the bottle so that more spice would come out. This was a very creative idea because it could be easily implemented. You can judge for yourself to see whether there was an element of "cheating" here. It certainly dovetailed well with this stratagem.

Stratagem No. 2: Besiege Wei to rescue Zhao (*wei Wei jiu Zhao*, 围魏救赵)

This stratagem means to surround one state to save another. The two warring parties, Wei and Zhao, each sent its best troops to fight in a battle, leaving behind the old and the sick. Zhao's army was advised to attack the old and the sick in the state of Wei from the back. In this way, Wei's troops would give up attacking Zhao and rush back to rescue their people.

The state of Zhao had two advantages: firstly, the state was not under attack, and secondly, its army could have reached the state of Wei ahead to besiege it. This is to surround one state to save another, or to relieve the besieged by besieging the base of the besiegers.

In life, you have to be aware that people who make use of this tactic are good at avoiding the important and harping on the trivial. They will subtly make an empty show of strength and keep silent about major changes while admitting minor ones. It also teaches you not to give up hope easily. If you have been sincere and generous to others, you could be the Zhao rescued by them when you are in need of help.

Stratagem No. 3: Murder with a borrowed knife (*jie dao sha ren*, 借刀殺人)

This stratagem makes use of another person to get rid of an adversary without you having to lift a finger. While the enemy emerges and becomes a threat, another powerful force is in the making. You should then make full use of this force to eliminate your enemy. By relying on others to defeat your enemy, you conserve your own strength. You "murder with a borrowed knife."

During the 1997 financial crisis, the Hong Kong dollar was under speculative pressure. The United Kingdom was handing over sovereignty of Hong Kong to China. Initially, the Hong Kong Monetary Authority (HKMA) managed to protect the currency against speculators trying to take advantage of the situation. However, when things turned from bad to worse, the HKMA sought the help and backing of the Beijing government. Owing to this, the HKMA was able to emerge a winner in its war against financial speculators. In this case, the HKMA had "murdered" the speculators with a "borrowed knife," which was China.

In business, this stratagem is often applied by borrowing the comparative advantages of others to defeat your opponent. In the 1970s, the British were reluctant to give Singapore Airlines (SIA) landing rights in London, even though a British airline could land in Singapore. A slowdown on servicing British Airways jets was then mounted by the National Trades Union Congress (NTUC) of Singapore; within weeks, SIA was given the landing rights in London. (Lee Kuan Yew 2000: 229) SIA had thus "murdered" London with a "borrowed knife" from the NTUC.

Stratagem No. 4: Wait at ease for an exhausted enemy (*yi yi dai lao*, 以逸待勞)

An army general well versed in the art of war will avoid as far as possible clashing head-on with an enemy that is high in morale. He will tire his opponents out by keeping them on the run. At the same time, the general will consolidate his army before attacking the exhausted opponents, who would soon become impatient. This is facing the weary in a relaxed mood.

When you send others on a wild goose chase to make them disheartened, you will be in a very comfortable situation to strike a deal in your favour. When you wait at ease, you will find the opportune moment to go into action. You strike back when the timeliness, the geographical position, and the support of the people are on your side. While waiting, you also prepare yourself for any eventuality.

This stratagem requires you to be in an invincible position and to think and act with foresight. In order to defeat your enemies, you must be in control of the whole situation and lead them by the nose. You are the one to call the tune as and when you need. In this way, you are at ease, waiting for your exhausted enemies to be submissive to you. You need therefore to plan ahead so as not to be in a frantic rush in times of emergency. If you are proactive while your enemies are reactive, you forestall them.

Stratagem No. 5: Looting a burning house (*chen huo da jie*, 趁火打劫)

A group of bandits saw someone's house on fire and went into it to pull off a robbery. They took away whatever property they could lay their hands on. The master of the house then reprimanded the bandits, who had the cheek to reply, "We are just trying to help you send these things to our house for safekeeping." This was how "looting a burning house" came about to mean taking advantage of the misfortune of others. In any negotiation, if you try to impose harsh terms on the other party because of your slight edge, you are looting the burning house.

If you are working in the financial sector, it pays to study how certain speculators make money using this stratagem. The British pound crisis in 1992, the bond market and Mexican crisis in 1994, the Asian financial disaster in 1997, and the oil price speculation in the 2000s are good lessons to be learnt. You ought therefore to take preventive measures in your planning so that you give others no chance to use this stratagem on you.

The modified version of this stratagem is that opportunity does not strike twice. You will not find yourself in the midst of a burning house. You have to be at the right time and the right place. Hence, when there is a golden opportunity for you to achieve your goal, seize it so that success can be reached.

Stratagem No. 6: Feint east, strike west (*sheng dong ji xi*, 声東击西)

A feint is a pretended attack or blow to distract an opponent's attention from the main attack. A boxer may make a feint with one hand only to strike his opponent forcefully with the other. In warfare, this feint can be an empty show of strength. The sound of attack may be in the east, but you strike in the west. Your opponent will be confused as to your next move.

People may spread false information about their intention, thereby diverting their opponent's attention. They do it so they have the opportunity to strike at the vulnerable front of an opponent. As no one knows their hidden agenda, they gain an extra advantage by unfair means. They profit at other people's expense.

During the Vietnam War, also known as the Second Indochina War (1959-1975), the full deployment of this stratagem was demonstrated by the Vietnamese Communists, who made the American forces playing hide-and-seek with them. The guerrilla fighters disguised themselves among the local populace, could vanish within minutes of an attack, and appeared at any moment in an ambush.

The American soldiers were always in the open while the guerrilla fighters were in hiding, so the Americans were under constant psychological pressure of being attacked, be it in towns, villages, jungles, paddy fields, or river deltas. As the Chinese saying goes, "The dragon which crosses the river is no match for the snake in its old haunts"; the Americans finally lost the war to the guerrilla fighters, who had the edge of knowing well the topography of their land.

Defending Stratagems

Stratagem No. 7: Making something out of nothing (*wu zhong sheng you*, 无中生有)

Laozi was the first philosopher of Daoism in ancient China. To him, all things under heaven existed from something, and something that existed came out of nothing. Under this stratagem, the action of telling lies cannot go on for long, because the truth will ultimately prevail. "Nothing" is used to confuse the enemy, while "exist" is the real intention, disguised in false impression. When you make something out of nothing, you mix the spurious with the genuine to deceive others.

An old Chinese tale about a tiger appearing in a busy street being accepted to be true when told by three persons is a good example of this stratagem. A minister asked his king, "If a person reports to you that there is a tiger in the street, would Your Majesty believe it?" "How can a tiger roam in the street? I don't believe it," answered the king. The minister then asked again, "If two persons were to come and report that a tiger is in the street, would Your Majesty believe it?" The king then replied, "If there are two persons saying the same thing, then I may believe it half-heartedly."

"What if three persons say the same thing to Your Majesty?" the minister asked. "If that is the case, then I have to believe it," replied the king. The minister then said, "No tiger will just walk on a busy street. Your Majesty will believe it because three persons tell you the same piece of news. Now that I am going away with the prince, I believe that there could be more than three persons who would slander me behind my back. I beg Your Majesty to be careful of what they might say about me." The king nodded, saying, "I know what you mean. Just set out on your journey and don't worry." True enough, there were many talebearers who spread spiteful gossip to the king about the minister. Before long, the king began to believe in them. "Three persons talking about a tiger make it real" applies in this case. (Baidu 2008b)

The moral in this stratagem is that you must learn to differentiate the truth from hearsay; rumours must stop at the wise. Gossip mongers, who are fond of telling tales, tend to make something out of nothing to impress their listeners. In office politics, using this stratagem to run someone down is a common practice. Let there be no falsehood in your speech, and you will be respected as a person of integrity.

There is a widespread story regarding a Scottish farmer who saved the life of a drowning boy but refused to be rewarded by the boy's grateful father. The boy's father then offered to pay for the education of the farmer's son. The village boy grew up to be Sir Alexander Fleming, who discovered penicillin. As fate would have it, years later the nobleman's son, who once escaped death, was now stricken with pneumonia. The penicillin saved the nobleman's son. The name of the nobleman was Lord Randolph Churchill and his son, Sir Winston Churchill. (TruthOrFiction. com 1998-2008) This story is not true but someone has made something out of nothing. If you are wise, you will not believe in a story that has not been substantiated with facts.

Stratagem No. 8: Cross Chencang in the dark (*an du chencang*, 暗渡陈倉)

Chencang was an ancient city. When you cross Chencang in the dark, you do things in secret. You can then expect some backlash when the cat is let out of the bag. A person may set up a false front to distract his enemies before attacking on their weakest defence; his hidden agenda is his secret weapon. This is a common tactic in business dealings or at share markets where consumers or investors who are not wary of false information created by inside trading can lose their money. If you are a person who is aboveboard, you will do nothing underhanded. Hence, you must be vigilant if you are in the open while your enemy is in hiding.

This stratagem is also used to describe those who are unfaithful to their spouses by engaging in secret rendezvous. They are ashamed of their deeds and so cannot date one another openly. They may mix the spurious with the genuine, pretending that they are on official duty away from home when they are actually on a date. Things that cannot be achieved through the proper channels therefore have to be done secretly.

This stratagem applies also to secret talks between opposition leaders looking to unite the two parties without the knowledge of the grass root supporters. There may be plans for the two parties to work closely with each other or be merged. The secret meetings would come to light only when the newspapers report the secret backroom deals after the fact; when the leaders are questioned and challenged, more inside stories will be unveiled publicly. There would then be different voices about the direction in which both parties should go.

Stratagem No. 9: Watch a fire from the other side of the river (*ge an guan huo*, 隔岸观火)

This is similar to sitting on top of the mountain to watch the tigers fight or looking on at somebody's misfortune with indifference. A person may calmly look on others to fight their way out through their internal troubles. Since he is watching the fire from afar, he can be sure that he will not be burnt. After watching the internal conflicts of the warring parties as clearly as a blazing fire, he will then reap the spoils when both parties are exhausted.

In 1994, genocide occurred in Rwanda, resulting in the mass killing of 800,000 minority Tutsis and majority Hutus in less than a hundred days. The systematic massacre occurred while the international community closed its eyes. (SciCentral 2005-2008) The crisis of ethnic and tribal conflicts in Darfur Sudan reared its ugly head in 2003, leaving 400,000 dead and forcing two million people to flee their country. (Le Monde Diplomatique 2008) Apparently the world has not learnt any lesson from the civil war in Rwanda to be proactive enough to prevent the deepening crisis in Darfur. Those who could help were watching a fire from the other side of the river; too little had been done, too late.

Stratagem No. 10: Hide a dagger in a smile (*xiaoli cang dao,* 笑里藏刀)

People who look meek and gentle outwardly may have murderous intent behind their smile. You need to nurture yourself into someone who is magnanimous; do not apply this stratagem in your life, because it is sinister and ruthless. Out of the thirty-six stratagems, this one is the most commonly used and is difficult for opponents to detect. When people want to climb the corporate ladder through stabbing one another's back, you can expect the so-called smiling true friends to turn out to be devils in disguise.

You may fall into the trap of this stratagem if you have vanity and like people to flatter you. Many ancient kingdoms fell because the leaders were surrounded by advisers who had daggers behind their smiles. The advisers were honey-mouthed and dagger-hearted. You need to learn to differentiate between sinister smiles and genuine ones.

As William Shakespeare (1564-1616) wrote in *Macbeth* (act 2, scene 3), "There's daggers in men's smiles; the near in blood, the nearer bloody." This part of a line was spoken by Donalbain to Malcom, the sons of Duncan, the king of Scotland. After murdering Duncan, Macbeth killed the king's sons, to do away with witnesses. Macbeth then falsely accused others of Duncan's murder. Macbeth's hypocrisy in showing his great grief was seen through by Donalbain, who noted that there were daggers in men's smiles.

Stratagem No. 11: A plum dying for a peach (*li dai tao jiang*, 李代桃僵)

This stratagem signifies the sacrifice made by one tree for another. It originated from a passage regarding the selflessness of a plum tree manifested in its dying for a peach tree. A peach tree was growing in an open air near a courtyard, and a plum tree was growing just next to it. Insects came to attack the peach tree. The plum tree came to the rescue of the peach tree and allowed itself to be tortured to death.

If a tree could fall for another and sacrifice itself for another, why could it not among friends or colleagues? In the business world, individual sacrifices may have to be made for a greater goal to be achieved. However, this may involve an innocent party being sacrificed in the scapegoat strategy.

Have you ever seen a lizard with no tail? It is the natural instinct of a lizard to shed its tail when it is in danger. This will cause its enemy to be temporarily distracted and focus on the tail while it runs away; the lizard sacrificed its tail to save its life. This illustrates that in life, you have to make some sacrifices in order to preserve what is vital.

Shakespeare's *Romeo and Juliet* is the well-known story of two young lovers' struggle against fate and fortune, which forced them to commit suicide in despair. At the end of the play,

Romeo drank the poison he had purchased and died kissing Juliet, thinking that she was already dead, when in actual fact she was not. When Juliet awoke to see her lover dead beside her, she killed herself with his dagger. Romeo and Juliet were willing to die for each other.

Stratagem No. 12: Conveniently lead away a goat (*shun shou qian yang*, 順手牽羊)

A man walked calmly through a flock of goat, leading one away by hand. This stratagem means to walk off with something or picking up something on the way. There is no pre-planning for this stratagem to take place; one just grasps the opportunity that appears out of the blue. This calls for sharp observation and the ability to be proactive.

During the period of the Three Kingdoms (220-280), an intelligent eight-year-old boy by the name of Zhu Ge Ke followed his father to a banquet hosted by the emperor. The distinguished guests at the feast deliberately asked the boy difficult questions to test his forte. They all marveled at his intelligence as he answered all questions. The emperor then secretly asked one of his eunuchs to bring in a donkey to the dining hall. There was a commotion when the guests saw the donkey, which had a paper stuck to its forehead; on the paper were written four Chinese characters: "Zhu Ge Zi Yu."

When a high ranking military officer read out the words, the whole hall was filled with roaring laughter. The characters on the donkey's paper insinuated that the father of the young boy looked like a donkey, which was a great insult. However, the young boy demonstrated his talent when he walked over to the emperor and said, "Is it Your Highness's intention to give this donkey to my father?" The emperor then smiled and said, "How do you know that I intend to give this donkey to your father as a reward?"

The young boy then said with great poise, "My father has always been honest and tolerant. He has gained the trust of Your Highness so much so that you would reward him with a donkey in front of all the distinguished guests." The emperor then told the boy to give him one good reason why the donkey was meant for his father and not for someone else.

The young boy then asked for a brush from a eunuch and added two characters at the end of the four words, making the paper now read: "Zhu Ge Zi Yu's donkey." Everybody laughed heartily, and the emperor then commended the boy for his quick-wittedness, allowing him to lead the donkey away. (Wang Guang Zhao and Lu Rong 1994: 682-684) The young boy made use of this stratagem to save his father from embarrassment. He might not have led away a goat, but a donkey was just as good in this instance.

Attacking Stratagems

Stratagem No. 13: Beat the grass and frighten away the snake (*da cao jing she*, 打草惊蛇)

When villagers walk through bushes, they will beat the grass with a stick to frighten away hidden snakes. This is to safeguard themselves from being bitten by poisonous snakes. Any snake on the path will also be killed. The wisdom of this stratagem is that before you embark on any business strategy, do not let the cat out of the bag, or else your opponent may come to know about it and spoil your plan.

There was a government officer who was obsessed with money. One day, the people of the county joined force to petition for action to be taken against his secretary for corruption. When the officer realised that the charges against his secretary had implications for himself, he felt like a frightened snake in the grass. Similarly, if the head of a department is arrested and prosecuted for corruption, the subordinates who work hand-in-glove with him will also be frightened, knowing that their days may be numbered.

Share markets are very sensitive to information, especially secrets coming through the grapevine. Speculators who are well-versed in the psychological warfare will not be easily influenced into buying and selling their shares. There is always a mixture of truth and falsehood in rumours. A negative remark made on the economy of a country by the authorities, for example, may frighten away foreign investors.

This stratagem can also be used to protect trade secrets, which can be vital to a company. They can be in the forms of statistics, designs, recipes, databases, or marketing strategies. If the secrets are leaked out, the competitors will make use of the information obtained for their own use. In your course of duty, you ought to take every precaution to make sure there is confidentiality in the trade secrets of your company. Avoid beating the grass and frightening away the snake, or else your competitors will be so frightened as to take immediate countermeasures to beat you in your own game.

Stratagem No. 14: Borrow a corpse to bring back a spirit (*jie shi huan hun*, 借尸还魂)

This means to raise a corpse from the dead. It means you do not use things that are useful to others. Instead, you use things that others are not using. This can mean making full use of something that has not been used through neglect or is considered obsolete. When you make use of ideas considered useless by others to achieve your aim, you are borrowing a corpse to bring back a spirit. The beauty of this stratagem is that when you make use of something that seems useless, others will not be suspicious of your action.

This stratagem may also be implied when people of lesser ability are hired by an employer who does not want to be outshined. You will learn that in life, you should never be smarter than your boss; as a culture, we have inculcated tends to reward the incompetent and neglect the stars. On the other hand, a person fallen in grace may appoint someone close to him to take over his place to make sure that there is still an influence by proxy. This stratagem makes use of the influential external forces to stage a comeback.

During the Tang dynasty (618-907), Pei Lue could turn defeat into victory by using this stratagem. After he failed an examination meant for military officials, Pei went to see the prime minister, whom the family had casual acquaintance with. Pei was allowed into the prime minister's office, but the Minister of Defence happened to be there as well. Pei immediately realised that the visitation was wrongly timed.

Nevertheless, the topic of failing the examination was brought up by Pei, who lamented that the examiners could have been drunk and just omitted his name from the passing list. After some conversation, the prime minister then pointed at the screen dividing the hall and asked Pei to compose a poem. Pei then walked to the screen and started reciting:

> Eight, nine feet in height,
> Six, seven steps the strides;
> Suddenly sit blocking the hall,
> Many a talent has thou mauled.

Pei then raised his voice and shouted, "Now that the most honourable is here opening up four doors to welcome the talented from far and wide, who are you to prevent them from coming in?" As soon as Pei had finished with his words, he pushed the screen to the ground. His poem implied that the authorities did not have the wisdom to make full use of capable people. Instead, they had obstructed them from serving the country. Pei's resourcefulness earned him a post as a junior officer. (Dong Boyong and Chen Li 1994: 487-490) The screen served as the corpse, in paving the way for Pei to start his official career.

Stratagem No. 15: Lure the tiger out of the mountains (*diao hu li shan*, 調虎离山)

The tiger is a much feared animal which would be difficult to deal with face to face on its home ground. However, if it is lured out of the mountain to the flatlands, the chances of defeating the tiger are much better. Similarly, when you lure your business competitor away from his base, you are inducing him to come out of his stronghold. By avoiding a head-on collision with your powerful rival, coupled with the strategy of diverting his attention, he will have to compromise with you on your terms. This stratagem means to stay clear of your rival's main force and strike at his weak points.

William Shakespeare's *Julius Caesar* described a plan by the enemies of Caesar to lure him from his house to be assassinated. While Caesar was ready to go to the Senate, his wife begged him not to go, because she had had nightmares that his statue was covered with blood, and she saw smiling men bathing their hands in the blood. Caesar did not take heed of his wife's warnings and departed for the Senate in the company of the conspirators.

As Caesar headed for the Senate, someone handed him a letter warning him about the conspirators. Caesar, however, did not read it immediately. At the Senate, the conspirators spoke to Caesar, bowing at his feet and encircling him as if to manifest their loyalty and respect for him. At this juncture, Caesar was repeatedly stabbed by his conspirators. When the dying Caesar saw his close friend Brutus among his murderers, he gave up his struggle against the killers, who had indeed bathed their hands and swords in Caesar's blood.

The stratagem used by the conspirators was to lure the tiger out of the mountains so that Caesar (the tiger) was at the mercy of his traitors.

Stratagem No. 16: To capture, you need to set free (*yu qin gu zong*, 欲擒故纵)

This stratagem calls for a person to act against the norm so that his aim is achieved. In order to enlarge, you need to contract; in order to weaken, you need to strengthen; in order to take, you need to give first. Enemies on the run may turn back to strike at you desperately. However, if they are let loose for a while, they may scatter and be taken captive without further resistance. To capture, therefore, is the end, and to set free is the means. Thus, the ends justify the means. It is important to know that this stratagem calls for good timing to succeed.

There was a scholar who passed his imperial examination and was about to be posted as an officer in a notorious state, where the minting of fake copper coins was rampant. The ringleader was a bandit who supervised cronies far and wide to run the illegal activities. Besides living this licentious life, he also employed a group of gangsters to bribe government officials, who would then tell him which informers should be killed.

The scholar was saddened and vowed to get rid of this evil force. He then summoned all his officers and people to inform them that if he could not apprehend the local tyrants, he would tender his resignation as the officer of the state. Furthermore, he issued a statement that minting fake copper coins was a serious offence and that anyone who could provide information leading to the arrest of the culprits would be rewarded.

The scholar knew very well that the culprit had controlled the local strategic points for many years; he was a local villain, or a snake in its old haunts. The only way to overcome the enemy is by strategy, not by forceful attack. After the message was spread all over the state, he just sat in his office, waiting for the informers to come. True enough, there were many informers because of the handsome reward. However, they were all publicly chastised by the scholar for giving him the wrong information.

The scholar's inconsistency gave the people the idea that he was not really serious in purging his state of criminals. This further fueled the unbridled activities of the ringleader and his accomplices. After some time, a few more informers came to report that they had caught two suspects minting fake copper coins. The scholar was not perturbed at this; he merely had the criminals questioned before jailing them.

All the activities of the scholar had been monitored by the "eyes and ears" of the ringleader, who then concluded that the scholar was just a toothless tiger; he assumed that his underlings could be released if he were to bribe the scholar. Without much thought, the ringleader approached the scholar to offer his bribe but was caught red-handed. When news of the ringleader's capture was spread all over the state, more than a hundred people came forward with concrete proof of his evil deeds. The villain pleaded guilty and was sentenced to death, while more than two hundred of his accomplices were jailed. (Wang Guang Zhao and Lu Rong 1994: 820-822) It was the stratagem of the scholar to set the ringleader free first before capturing him.

Stratagem No. 17: Cast a brick to attract jade (*pao zhuan yin yu*, 抛砖引玉)

This stratagem means to offer general remarks by way of introduction so that others may come up with their own opinions. You present your findings to attract other learned parties to come out with their findings, which should have more breadth and depth. This stratagem does not sound evil, like *Looting a burning house* or *Murder with a borrowed knife.* It can be applied in both the positive and negative aspects.

A parent who donates generously to a school building fund may encourage other parents to do so by casting the brick. On the other hand, an illegal money-lender may offer a very attractive package deal in return for exorbitantly high interest rates. In order to make this stratagem effective, the brick must be hurled only once and at the right time for the impact to be felt.

Brainstorming is used to gather information or generate ideas. During the brainstorming sessions, participants are encouraged to contribute as many ideas about a specific issue as they can think of. Generally, discussion leaders will put their ideas on the floor to initiate active participation and discuss the subject matter in detail. You may not be the only expert in your field, so this stratagem, which allows participants to come out with the best innovative solution to a problem, will also benefit you greatly. The contributions of your colleagues may inspire you to see things from a different perspective.

Stratagem No. 18: To catch bandits, first catch the ringleader (*qin zei xian qin wang*, 擒賊先擒王)

When you want to catch a person, shoot at his horse first; and to catch bandits, first catch their ringleader. The rider would fall together with the horse, while the bandits will scatter when their ringleader is captured. In problem solving, you must identify where the crux of the matter is. All problems can be solved when you tackle them at their source.

These are the bandits in your heart: if you procrastinate and do not meet the deadlines of your work; are sarcastic towards your friends and colleagues; are jealous of their achievements; are constantly creating problems in the office;

are not interested in attending training courses; or are arrogant and quick-tempered. The ringleader of these bandits will then be your negative attitude. However, once you are positive and proactive, all your weaknesses will disappear because their ringleader has been caught. If you recall chapter 1, then this stratagem has to do with "knowing your enemy."

As the Chinese adage goes, when the tree falls, the monkeys scatter. This means when an influential person falls from power, his hangers-on disperse. The analogy is that when a company loses a capable leader, it loses its direction, just like a boat without a rudder. It is also said that when you strike a snake, strike at the seven-inch position of the head where its heart, the vital organ, is. When its heart stops beating, the snake will not strike back. If you hit the head of the snake, its tail will strike at you, and if you hit its tail, it will turn to bite you. This stratagem therefore calls for a quick, effective, and decisive action to tackle problems at source once and for all.

Summary

A stratagem is a plan to deceive the enemy; the Greeks used the wooden horse as a stratagem to capture Troy. In ancient China, the thirty-six stratagems were referred to as the art of war, and they are now being used in marketing as crafty tricks which are abhorrent to honest businessmen. As such, the thirty-six stratagems can be viewed as a double-edged sword. They are necessary at the pivotal moment of war but are considered unscrupulous when used unethically in business and social circles.

The thirty-six stratagems are grouped into six sets. This chapter discusses the first three sets to be used when one has a slight edge over others; the other three, used when one is at a disadvantage, will be discussed in the following chapter. The first set of six winning stratagems include *Murdered with a borrowed knife, Wait at ease for an exhausted enemy,* and *Looting a burning house*; defending stratagems include *Making something out of nothing, Hiding a dagger in a smile,* and *A plum dying for a peach.* In the third set of the six stratagems, you are told on how to *Beat the grass and frighten away the snake, Lure the tiger out of the mountains,* and *To capture, you need to set free.*

These eighteen stratagems can be applied when your enemy is at your mercy. You have the privilege to call the tune.

Chapter Six

Understanding the Thirty-Six
Stratagems (Part II)

Stratagems to be used when one is at a disadvantage

Chaos Stratagems

Stratagem No. 19: Take away the firewood from under the cauldron (*fu di chou xin*, 釜底抽薪)

A cauldron is a large metal pot for boiling liquids over a fire. It was commonly used in ancient China. When the firewood is taken away from under the cauldron, it signifies that a drastic measure has been taken to deal with a situation.

In dealing with an opponent whose strength is as powerful as the boiling water and the fierce fire, it is not advisable for you to confront him directly. You are not likely to withstand his attack. The best strategy for you then is to take away the firewood from under the cauldron so that the fire is not there to boil the water. In this way, the strength of your opponent will be greatly reduced. The firewood is the key to solving the problem. You have to be creative in thinking of a way to remove the firewood.

You might have learnt in history about Napoleon Bonaparte (1769-1821), emperor of the French, whose defeat at the Battle of Waterloo marked the end of his final bid for power. That battle also marked the beginning of the end of the Hundred Days, Napoleon's attempt at regaining his glorious past. At one point, when the Russians were unable to stop the French forces, they employed the stratagem of removing all food supplies from the city of Moscow before retreating. Without food, the French soldiers would have no energy to fight the battle. The Russians had effectively taken away the firewood from under the cauldron. Besides, Napoleon was also defeated by the bitter cold of winter.

Stratagem No. 20: Fish in troubled waters (*hun shui mo yu*, 浑水摸鱼)

When the water is clear, the fishes will be able to see their enemies approaching clearly and hide themselves in time. However, when the bottom of the river is stirred up and the water turns murky, the fishes will just flee in all directions into the hands of their captors. This is common knowledge among fishing enthusiasts.

You are stirring up the waters to catch fish when you take advantage of a chaotic situation. History abounds with stories of heroes emerging in troubled times. When the situation is at sixes and sevens in a competitive setting, the one who is decisive and pragmatic takes the crown. Investors who buy up shares of companies running into financial difficulties temporarily may be fishing in troubled waters, befitting the old notion that fish bite more readily when waters are rough.

This stratagem has always been used by politicians attempting to reap the benefits of political instability. Politicians who have no principle will always fish in troubled waters, hopping like grasshoppers from one political party to another. They are crafty and know when to trim their sails.

This stratagem is often deployed by market competitors who outwit one another by offering relatively lower prices to consumers. In the price war that ensues, the less efficient and competitive businesses will be edged out of the market, thereby allowing the surviving competitors to share the economic cake left over by the losers in the troubled waters.

Stratagem No. 21: The gold cicada slips out of its skin (*jin chan tuo ke*, 金蟬脫壳)

A cicada is a tropical insect with large transparent wings that makes a high singing noise. When a person slips out of a predicament, like a gold cicada sloughing its skin, he is escaping by putting up a false front. This stratagem calls for quick-wittedness in a crisis to head off a disaster. You need to retreat at times in order to advance and to make concessions in order to gain advantages. President and Mrs Marcos of the Philippines fled the country in 1986. In their hurry to escape the wrath of the people, Mrs Marcos left behind 1,220 pairs of shoes at the presidential palace. (BBC 1999)

Another classic example of this stratagem is that of Alberto Kenya Fujimori (1938-present), the president of Peru from 1990 to 2000. His parents moved to Peru in 1934, and Fujimori was born in Lima. He was forced to flee to Japan when allegations of his involvement in corruption emerged. Fujimori then sent his letter of resignation by fax from Japan, but the Peruvian Congress rejected his resignation and removed him from office. (Japan 101.com 2003-2005). However, in 2007, Fujimori was finally extradited to face criminal charges in Peru and was sentenced to six years in prison. The Supreme Court rejected his appeal on April 15, 2008.

When you are surrounded by competitors, you need to think of a way to break out of the encirclement. You can modify this stratagem to suit your situation. For example, you may employ the blue ocean strategy by going into areas where others have not ventured. Opportunities abound beyond the boundary of a nation.

Stratagem No. 22: Lock the door to catch the thief (*quan men zhuo zei*, 关門捉賊)

You lock the door so that the thief in your house cannot escape. In fighting battles, you catch invading enemies by not letting them get away. You prevent them from going back to their base with what they have taken from you. When they are cornered, they will have to surrender.

During the Tang dynasty (AD 618-907), there was an orphan who was worried about his six cattle when he was called up for the national service. He then decided to pay his uncle to take care of them while he was away. As time went by, thirty calves were born.

When the orphan came home after his national service to collect his cattle, he was told by his uncle that two of his cattle had died and he could take home the other four. However, when the orphan saw the thirty calves at the cattle pen, he knew what was in the mind of his uncle. Nevertheless, after being told that the thirty calves were not his, the orphan went away angrily and reported the matter to Pei Ziyun, the magistrate.

Pei then ordered the arrest of the uncle for having stolen the thirty calves. The uncle panicked and went to the magistrate to clear his name. A witness, whose face was covered, was then brought in to testify against the uncle, who was forced to admit his guilt. Pei then ordered the witness to remove his face cover, revealing him to be the orphan and putting his uncle to shame. (Dong Boyong and Chen Li 1994: 472-475) The magistrate had brilliantly made use of the stratagem by cornering the culprit in the courtroom.

Stratagem No. 23: Befriend distant allies, attack nearby (*yuan jiao jing gong,* 远交近攻)

When you are more likely to be attacked by those nearby, you attack those nearby while making allies at a distance. Very often, the faithful old guards in a company are replaced by newcomers so that the position of the one in power will not be threatened. This is another form of befriending distant allies while attacking those nearby.

This stratagem can be deployed in a business alliance made out of geographical necessity. The alliance with a well-known business associate in a faraway place can be strengthened to ward off the threat of nearby competitors through co-branding. In terms of military strategy, a small nation may ally itself with a distant superpower to safeguard itself from being attacked by its neighbouring countries.

In politics, there is no lasting friendship or lasting enmity, and it is the field where common enemies make allies. In business, all is self-interest, while in social circles, friendship is just a matter of convenience. Genuine friendship is rare, and this has prompted us to always say that dog is man's best friend. To quote Mark Twain, "If you pick up a starving dog and make him prosperous, he will not bite you. This is the principal difference between a dog and a man."

When this stratagem is reversed, modified, and applied in our daily life, it implies that charity begins at home and we should start loving our family members first before we do so to others. Do not seek far and wide for what lies close at hand.

Stratagem No. 24: Borrow a route to conquer Guo (*jia tu fa Guo*, 假途伐虢)

Guo was a state in ancient China. This stratagem signifies an army which borrowed the right of way to attack its neighbour. In the business world, a company which faces financial crisis or a consumer boycott may employ this stratagem by having social and welfare activities as an avenue to gain back the trust and confidence of its customers.

In the early 1960s, the hippie subculture was a youth movement that originated in the United States and spread around the world. Hippies were anti-establishment, critical of middle-class values, and opposed nuclear weapons and the Vietnam War. (Wikipedia 2008d) They took drugs and looked unkempt. It was an era when young people felt depressed, were at the crossroads, and wanted love. It was at this time that Brian Samuel Epstein unknowingly applied this stratagem to bring hope and inspiration to the wayward young people through the Beatles. This pop group from Liverpool consisted of John Lennon, Paul McCartney, George Harrison, and Ringo Starr.

In 1961, Epstein was a twenty-seven-year-old proprietor of Liverpool's popular North End Music Store when he discovered the talented Beatles. It started when music lovers asked for the record for the single "My Bonnie," which was available in Germany but not in Britain. He offered to be the manager for the Beatles, who were overjoyed at the offer. (*Moment Magazine* 2007-2008)

Having received the confidence of the Beatles, Epstein recast their image by giving them a new hair style and tailored suits. He wanted them to look clean and tidy and to act like professionals. The Beatles were an international success, and they derived inspiration and self-confidence from their manager. The Beatles struck a sympathetic chord with young people around the world. Epstein was the genius who had re-engineered and inculcated the positive values of having self-esteem and neat-looking appearance among the youth. He had aptly employed the stratagem of borrowing the talent of the Beatles to conquer pessimism and low morale of the hippie subculture.

Merging Stratagems

Stratagem No. 25: Steal a beam to replace a pillar (*tou liang huan zhu*, 偷樑換柱)

The alternate translation from the original Chinese version is "Steal the beams and pillars and replace them with rotten timber." It signifies perpetrating a fraud through misrepresentation. This is done when an opponent is in a state of confusion. When he comes to his senses, it will be too late for him to reverse the situation.

In the Chinese idiom "Calling a stag a horse," Prime Minister Zhao wanted to know which ministers were supporting him and which were against him. One day he let someone bring a stag to the court and said to the emperor, "Your Majesty, here is a fine horse I am presenting to you." The emperor was puzzled and said, "Mr Prime Minister, this is a stag. Why do you say it is a horse?" The prime minister, however, insisted that it was not only a horse but a winged steed, a horse that could cover a thousand *li* (miles) a day. The emperor looked at the stag closely again and said, "How can the antlers be grown on the head of a horse?"

At this juncture, the prime minister raised his voice while pointing his finger at the ministers and said, "Your Majesty, you can ask the ministers if you do not believe me." The ministers were shocked at this statement. However, the body language and the facial expressions of the premier sent a message to them that something sinister was going on. The timid ministers who did not want to go against their conscience by telling lies kept quiet, while the ministers who fawned upon Zhao immediately voiced their support saying, "This is really a horse that covers a thousand *li* a day." (TravelChinaGuide 1998-2008) As expected, the dissenting ministers who held on to their sense of justice were severely punished.

In *The Emperor's New Clothes* by Hans Christian Andersen, the two tailors were swindlers provided imaginary clothes for the emperor, whose priority in life was to wear elegant clothes. When the emperor went on a procession, a child said, "The emperor is naked." The bystanders also agreed and said, "The boy is right! The emperor is naked!" The emperor, however, continued the procession under the illusion that those who could not see his new clothes were stupid. The two tailors can be said to have applied the stratagem on the emperor. In this case, the "beam" was represented by the clothes the emperor had taken off for the new suits to be fitted, while the "pillar" was the emperor's vanity.

In the business world, the producers who are guilty of software piracy and other copyright infringements are the masters of this stratagem.

Stratagem No. 26: Point at the mulberry and scold the locust (*zhi sang ma huai*, 指桑骂槐)

This stratagem means to point at one but abuse another, making oblique accusations. It uses the art of insinuation. When you do not blame others directly but indirectly through insinuation, you are applying this technique. A superior might want to scold his officer but finds it difficult to do so directly, so he chooses to reprimand another staff member. The officer would obviously know that he was the one deserving the scolding but could not retaliate because the superior did not mention his name. This stratagem is commonly used when there are conflicts of interest. Everyone will then try to drop hints that others are the guilty parties. This is pointing at the mulberry tree and scolding the locust tree.

If you are married, you have probably witnessed the strained relationship between a mother-in-law and a daughter-in-law. In the Asian culture, the woman married to the first son, more so if he is the only son in the family, is expected to stay under the same roof with her husband's family. However, when two women of different backgrounds see each other every day, conflicts between them are bound to arise. Generally, most of the conflicts will originate from the mother-in-law, who may feel that her son is no longer her son now that he is married to another woman. His love has now been shifted to his wife. As such, you need to have wisdom to keep this stratagem from rearing its ugly head in the family.

Stratagem No. 27: Feign insanity without going mad (*jia chi bu dian*, 假痴不顛)

You may feign foolishness without going mentally deranged. This is another trick to fool people into parting with their money.

Two brothers were standing outside their clothes shop, inviting passersby to come inside. They were both hard of hearing and often heard incorrectly. After the elder brother told a customer about how good a suit was, the person asked, "How much does it cost?" The brother attending to the customer then put his hand up to his ear and asked, "What did you say?" The customer repeated in a louder voice, "How much does this cost?" The brother said, "Did you ask how much? I'm sorry, I couldn't hear well. Let me ask my brother." He then turned to his younger brother and shouted at him, "How much does this cost?"

The younger brother stood up, glanced at the customer and the suit, and answered, "That'll be $72." The older brother smiled and told the customer, "Sir, $22." On hearing this, the customer paid quickly for the suit and hurried off, thinking that he had got a very good deal (the suit actually cost $12 and there was a profit of $10). The truth was that the hearing of the two brothers was normal. They only feigned deafness for petty advantage. They were so successful in their business that they could afford to send their three children for tertiary education. (Qiye Wangjing 2008) While a fool may occasionally hit on a good idea, the two brothers only feigned insanity, and they were full of ideas.

Stratagem No. 28: Climb the roof and take away the ladder (*shang wu chou ti*, 上屋抽梯)

You have a problem if someone removes your ladder after you have climbed onto the roof. The reverse is true when you take away the ladder when your enemy is up the roof. For this stratagem to work well, you must make sure that your ladder is properly positioned, and there must be a reason for your opponent to want to climb on the roof. The timing for removing the ladder is also vital, or else your opponent will come down in time to take away the profits you worked so hard to preserve. Your opponent will come down from the roof when he does not find what he wants, so this stratagem calls for quick action, thereby forcing a quick outcome.

When there is a crash in the share market, small investors are likely to be hit the hardest. Why do they lose the most in such a situation? Generally, small investors are followers, who lack the knowledge of stock markets. They invest in shares after reading newspaper articles or base their investment on the recommendations of friends (who themselves may not know much about the market). Inevitably they fall prey to ailing companies which give the public the false perception that they are heading for a better performance.

After small investors purchase the shares of such companies, they will suddenly find themselves at the losing end when the price drops sharply. They are latecomers, buying shares at a high price, and when there is a crash in the market, their hope of making a profit is shattered. They may want to wait for the market to bounce back to cut their losses, but it may be too late for them, especially if they do not have the holding power. Even if they can hold on to the shares, their money is tied to the market. Small investors are lured to climb the roof, followed by the removal of the ladder by the ailing companies, which have no obligation to explain why you are told to be on the roof.

Stratagem No. 29: To blossom on a tree (*Shu shang kai hua*, 树上开花)

The original meaning of "blossoming on a tree" refers to adorning a barren tree with artificial flowers to deceive people. The implication is that external forces have been used to demonstrate someone's strength. In our modern economy, companies use marketing strategies like advertisements, exhibitions, and endorsements by professionals to popularise their products' brand names.

During the 2008 Beijing Summer Olympics, we not only witnessed many sporting events, we also saw a competition by logo designers and corporate branding. The logos of branded products were viewed by the billions of television viewers throughout the Games. The sponsors involved invested millions and paid high premiums for the right to advertise, with the hope that consumers all over the world would buy their products.

As the host of the Olympics, China displayed its creativity during the opening and closing ceremonies to give the global TV audience a unique experience of the country's thousands of years of history and culture. No effort was spared to portray China as an ancient nation which stresses harmony: between humans and society, between people, between humans and nature, and between mind and body.

Without doubt, the Beijing Olympics in 2008 will be engraved in the minds of billions of people, just like other Olympiads which have gone into history. By and large, China's leaders used the stratagem of blooming on the tree.

Stratagem No. 30: Turn the guest into the host (*fan ke wei zhu*, 反客为主)

When a guest overstays his welcome, he tends to act like a host. The passive then becomes the active. Many of today's businesses are involved in the copyright issue, and it is very common to see those who pirate the intellectual rights of others make huge profits by actively pushing their imitation products.

This stratagem can also be seen from another angle, as shown in the Malay proverb of "Like the Dutch asking for land" ("*Seperti Belanda Meminta Tanah*"). The Dutch colonised Indonesia and Malacca (now a state in west Malaysia); they were guests who turned into hosts. The same goes for other Western countries, which colonised the Third World in the last millennium; they got the resources they wanted and turned themselves into hosts.

Two companies producing similar products or offering similar services often merge into one large company. The normal scenario is when a smaller company is taken over by a bigger one. The name of the smaller company usually disappears. For example, two banks may merge into one; such a merger often leads to concerns for the staff of the smaller company. If they were the hosts in their previous company, they would be the guests after the merger. The reverse is also true. The company which has a bigger share has thus become the host to the now defunct smaller company.

Retreating Stratagems

Stratagem No. 31: Use of a woman to ensnare a man (*mei ren ji*, 美人计)

This is one of the most effective traps to make a person fall. There is a Chinese saying relevant to this stratagem: "It is difficult for heroes to pass the barrier of beautiful women." As the spirit is willing and the flesh is weak, you will do well in life if you shun the beauty trap.

A classic example of this stratagem is Britain's Profumo affair. It involved Christine Keeler, an English model and showgirl who had an intimate relationship with both John Profumo, a British government minister, and Yevgeny Ivanov, a Soviet spy. Keeler used this stratagem, which cost Profumo his job and caused embarrassment to the British government. (Wikipedia 2008b)

Mata Hari (1876-1917) was a beautiful dancer and courtesan whose name has become a synonym for a seductive female spy. She was born to a Dutch family and left Holland with her husband to live in Java, Indonesia. After divorcing him, she moved to Paris, using the name "Mata Hari," which means "eye of the dawn" in Javanese (in the Malay language, it means the "sun"). She became a dancer in Paris, where she met many famous and powerful people. She was recruited as a French spy to find information from the German officers. However, Mata Hari was suspected by the French of being a double agent; she was convicted of treason and executed on 15 October 1917. (AOL 2008)

There are many stories of high-ranking officers who lose all their standing because their enemies applied this stratagem of using women to ensnare them. You must discipline yourself and not fall into this temptation.

Stratagem No. 32: Empty-city stratagem (*kong cheng ji*, 空城计)

This scheme is used to deceive the enemy by opening the gates of a weakly defended city. By presenting a bold front, a weak defence is concealed. There is psychological warfare involved in this stratagem. For example, as empty vessels make the most noise, they will try all ways to convince others that they are men of great learning. This is true for those who are poor and yet want to present themselves as rich.

During the Trojan War, the Greeks besieged Troy for ten years but failed to overcome its defences. Odysseus, the hero of Homer's *Odyssey* and known for his wisdom and shrewd resourcefulness, came up with a creative plan to conquer the city. He built a huge wooden horse and pretended to leave it behind, as if the army had given up fighting and gone home.

The Trojans joyfully brought the horse through the gates and into their city, after which they began celebrating their victory. They did not know that several Greek soldiers were hiding inside the horse, waiting to strike at night after the Trojan soldiers were drunk and asleep. When the Greeks came down from the horse, they opened the gates and let the rest of the army in. The city was then besieged by the Greeks, who burned it to the ground, killing all the Trojan men and enslaving all the Trojan women.

Odysseus' strategy was just the opposite of the empty-city stratagem. The Greeks deceived their enemy, the Trojans, by presenting a weak front: leaving behind the wooden horse and seeming to depart the area. The Greeks were actually ushered right into the strongly defended city by the Trojans.

Stratagem No. 33: Scheme with double agents (*fan jian ji*, 反间计)

Warring parties, or competing companies in the business world, try their best to learn their opponent's secrets while preserving their own. For example, fast food chains keep many of their recipes secret. In this stratagem, wrong information is often deliberately disclosed to confuse the enemies and their spies. Likewise, you may collude with an opponent's employees to get them to provide vital information for you.

The indigenous people of South America discovered the secrets of the cocoa bean more than three thousand years ago. When the Spanish conquered Mexico in 1521, they stole the Aztec recipe for *xocolatl*, a drink made with cocoa. The conquistadors introduced the cocoa drink to the Spanish court, where sugar or honey was added. This secret of cocoa was kept for more than a hundred years by the Spanish until the seventeenth century, when the use of cocoa spread throughout Europe.

In the 1820s, Coenraad Johannes van Houten of Holland introduced two important inventions: a method to produce powder and butter from cocoa, and a method to enhance cocoa's taste and colour. He paved the way for a development by the Englishman John Fry which made cocoa taste richer. In 1875, the Swiss chemist Henri Nestle invented milk chocolate. The wrapped chocolate bar was another Dutch invention. (Cocoa 2008) These types of conspiracies and underhanded acts are frequently used in the business world.

Stratagem No. 34: The ruse of self-inflicted injury (*ku rou ji*, 苦肉计)

This stratagem is a way to deceive your enemy and win his trust (albeit a painful one). It is against our nature to hurt ourselves physically while pursuing our goals. Nevertheless, this stratagem can easily earn the sympathy of people with a sense of pity.

In the early 1960s, the Buddhists in Vietnam were persecuted by government authorities. In protest, Buddhist monks doused themselves with petrol and lit themselves on fire in the street, making front-page news worldwide. This led to the subsequent downfall of the ruling party. The monks who chose suicide by immolation had indeed manifested the deployment of the plot of self-inflicted injury (or more appropriately in this case, self-inflicted death).

In modern-day conflicts between nations, suicide bombers often strike, creating terrible carnage and chaos. These bombers are often driven to act by their ideology. However, it cannot be denied that the stratagem of self-inflicted injury, and in this instance, also self-inflicted death, has now been used as a means to an end. This stratagem requires sacrifices on the part of those who use it. They must be willing to go through the physical affliction or even death for the stratagem to be effective.

Stratagem No. 35: Interlocking hoops (*lian huan ji*, 连环计)

In any warfare, one must have more than one strategy. To win a battle therefore requires several strategies which are like interlocking hoops. In business, this stratagem calls for a series of inter-related tactics. To ensure success, every strategy has a scheme of its own for maximum desired effect.

In March 2008, the live telecast of the Olympic torch being lit in Greece was briefly disrupted by pro-Tibet activists. The torch was to have been carried around the world through twenty countries before it reached Beijing for the opening of the Games.

Human rights' groups in all the cities where the Olympic torch was to pass called for a boycott of the Games. The timing and the strategy of the pressure groups were so well planned that they were like interlocking hoops. The stratagem was effective; with relatively little cost and effort, the call for Tibetan freedom was relayed by the international media. In trying to break the interlocking hoops, the Chinese government and Olympics supporters had to take desperate countermeasures. These included denouncing the protests as despicable and tarnishing the lofty Olympic spirit. Hence, teamwork is required for the interlocking hoops stratagem to work effectively.

Stratagem No. 36: Best to go away (*zou wei shang ji*, 走為上计)

You must learn when it is best for you to run away; sometimes, retreating is the best option. When you find yourself in an embarrassing or a chaotic situation, you can make use of this stratagem if it is the best choice. As the saying goes, "As long as the green mountains are there, one need not worry about firewood"; you can stage a comeback later on. On the other hand, when it comes to helping friends in need of assistance, we should not run away from our obligation.

Idi Amin Dada (1920-2003) employed this stratagem in order to save his life. He overthrew President Milton Obote in 1971 and became Uganda's military dictator until 1979. Amin called himself "a pure son of Africa," and the ethnic cleansing he ordered, and the expulsion of Asians who had controlled the country's economy, shocked the world during his reign. Obote once called Amin "the greatest brute an African mother has ever brought to life." President Jimmy Carter said events in Uganda during Amin's rule "disgusted the entire civilised world." Amin, who said that Hitler "was right to burn six million Jews," was himself responsible for the death of 100,000 to 300,000 Ugandans. (Amin Index 2008) When his life was threatened, he fled the country, living in exile in Saudi Arabia until his death. Out of the thirty-six stratagems, this last one seemed to be the best choice for Amin.

Summary

This chapter deals with the last eighteen of the thirty-six stratagems, which are to be used when one is at a disadvantage;

they can be divided into three sets of six stratagems each. The chaos stratagems include *Take away the firewood from under the cauldron*, *The gold cicada slips out of its skin*, and *Lock the door to catch the thief*; the merging stratagems include *Steal a beam to replace a pillar*, *Point at the mulberry and scold the locust*, and *Climb the roof and take away the ladder*; and the retreating stratagems include *Scheme with double agents*, *The ruse of self-inflicted injury*, and *Interlocking hoops*.

The relevant stories from both the East and the West are discussed to make you understand better how these strategies are applied in political and social-economic settings. The *Fish in troubled waters* stratagem enriches your general knowledge in that when you stir up the bottom of the clear water to make it muddy, the fishes will panic and flee in all directions into the hands of their captors. You may find it useful to remember the last of the thirty-six stratagems, *Best to go away*, and the example of Idi Amin. When his life was threatened, he fled to Saudi Arabia and lived there until his death. Indeed, when you equip yourself with the knowledge of the thirty-six stratagems, you will be better prepared to face the challenges in your workplace and in your social circle.

Chapter Seven

Fly the Extra Mile

Plutarch (AD 46-120) was a Greek historian, biographer, and essayist. He said, "The mind is not a vessel to be filled but a fire to be kindled." Success belongs to people who have a burning desire to succeed. They will motivate themselves by being proactive and positive in their mind-set. When you kindle the fire in your mind, you will do things which others are only thinking about.

For you to fly the extra mile, like a roc, you need an attitudinal change. Your role as a decision maker, your art of delegating, your ability to put your ideas across, and your wanting to make the most of your time are other factors which can lighten your burden and make your journey easy. "The journey of a thousand *li* begins with the first step," and because the beginning is always the most difficult, you have the choice of initiating your effort now or deferring your action. You have much to gain if you make up your mind to follow through on your plan. Always remember that procrastination is the thief of time. In order to fly the extra mile in life, I suggest that you take note of the following points:

Make Your Dream Come True

You may find the story about a foolish old man removing the mountains both interesting and refreshing.

An old man of almost ninety years was staying in a house facing two mountains, which obstructed his way. One day he called for a meeting with his family members and told them of his plan to remove the two mountains so that a road would be opened. Everybody agreed except his wife, who said, "How can you remove two great mountains when we can't even level a small mound with a few of us? Furthermore, where are you going to dump the rocks and the earth?" The other family members then said that they would move the rocks and the earth to the nearby seashore.

When they started work the next morning, a grey-beard who was known as the wise old man approached the foolish old man and said, "You are real silly! An old man like you can hardly pull out a few blades of grass. How are you going to level the mountains?" The foolish old man answered, "I think you yourself are the real fool. It is true that I am old and will not live to see the two mountains levelled. But when I die, my sons will continue the work. When they die, my grandsons, and their sons and grandsons will continue the work. A day will come when the mountains will be flattened. What makes you think that we can't remove the mountains?" The wise old man was silenced. (Sina.com 2008)

The foolish old man's strong desire in wanting to turn his dream into reality is a trait you should possess to make your plan work. When you sink the boats after crossing, this implies that you have the dogged determination to go on with your plan and never give up. Though the foolish old man wanted to level the mountains, his sons and grandsons and their descendants also needed the determination to carry on the work of removing the mountains. If the spirit is willing, the flesh must also be strong. When you have the will to be a doer of your plans, you must also act to make them work.

Sustained Effort

Mencius taught the importance of sustained effort. He advised people not to be "inwardly like a lion but outwardly like a lamb," to not have a fine start but a poor finish. During Mencius' time, the king of Qi was unpopular with the people. They did not think that he could rule with wisdom.

Mencius happened to tour the state of Qi when he heard of all the negative comments about the king. He then said, "This has nothing to do with a person being wise or not. I shall illustrate this with the growing of a plant. If you put the plant in the sun for one day and freeze it for ten days, even the plant with the most viability will not grow well. From what I see, there are very few people who can give warmth to the king, as I do. The moment I am away, those who want to freeze the king will swarm round him. Although the king of Qi may intend to do something for the people, he can hardly achieve his aim because too many around him give him the cold shoulder." (Baidu 2008d)

Mencius was once a tutor to the king of Qi. However, the king lacked concentration while studying, and so Mencius left him for another student. This shows that when you work hard for one day and do nothing for ten, you are working by fits and starts. Similarly, when you are enthusiastic about your plan for one day and give it the cold shoulder for ten, you are not going to succeed.

After Brian Boyle graduated high school in 2004, he was in a serious car accident that almost claimed his life and left him in a coma. For two months, he was on life support at a hospital. When he finally woke up, he was surrounded by medical equipment. He began a long, painful journey of recovery. He went through fourteen operations, thirty-six blood transfusions, and thirteen plasma treatments; he also lost a hundred pounds.

Brian had set three goals before the accident: He wanted to go to college, join the swim team, and compete in an Ironman triathlon. He had the willpower to make his dreams come true, despite all the obstacles in his way. Brian later entered college and became a college swimmer, after going through much suffering. His story is told in *Living Proof: Miracles Do Happen,* which should encourage you to trust in God and never give up on your dreams. Brian achieved his third goal in 2007 when he competed in the Ford Ironman World Championship; his story was aired on NBC's *Ironman* show. (Inspirational Peak 2007b)

The Miscellaneous Notes of the Western Capital, a series of stories by Gehong (AD 284-364) of the Eastern Jin dynasty in ancient China, included a story about someone whose determination to study was an example of motivation. Kuang Heng's family was so poor that there was no money for the family to buy candles. However, his neighbour was rich, and so his house was always brightly lit with candles.

Kuang Heng asked his neighbour to let him study in his house; when this request was turned down, he secretly made a hole in the common wall so that his neighbour's light could shine into his room to enable him to read. Using this method, he finished reading all his books. Kuang Heng knew that the neighbour had a good collection of books, and he next proposed to his neighbour that he would work for him free of charge. The rich man was bewildered and asked for an explanation. Kuang Heng then said, "I am willing to work for you so that I can borrow your books." The rich man was pleased to accept the offer. This was how Kuang Heng finally became a learned man. He excelled in his studies because he was diligent and resourceful. Most important of all, Kuang Heng was highly motivated, regardless of the obstacles and adverse circumstances he had to face.

Remove All Groundless Fears

One afternoon, my two grandchildren were glued to the TV watching Disney's hilarious movie *Chicken Little*; the title character was always warning others that "The sky is falling!" Chicken Little grouped together his hysterical band of misfit friends to work frantically to save the planet from complete destruction. This reminds me of the story of the man of Qi who was haunted by the fear that the sky might fall. This story was written by Liezi of the Han dynasty.

In this story, a man from Qi was worried that the sky was falling. His friend came to calm him, saying, "The sky is nothing but air, which you breathe in and exhale into the sky all day long. Why should you need to worry that the sky would fall?" The man then asked, "If the sky is just air, what about the sun, the moon, and the stars? Won't they fall from the sky?" The friend replied, "They are only shining and twinkling objects of air. Even if they were to fall, they won't hurt you." The man then asked, "What about the sinking earth?"

The friend said, "The earth is made up of solid earth that filled up all spaces until there are no more empty spaces left. If you stamp your feet on the ground all day, the earth is not going to sink. Why do you worry that the earth will sink?" On hearing this, the man was very happy and so was his friend. Though the explanation given by the friend might not be accurate, you are reminded nonetheless that in life you should remove all imaginary or groundless fears. To be successful in life, you must be resolute, fear no sacrifice, and surmount every difficulty.

Harbour No Evil Thoughts

It pays to treat others with sincerity and respect. You should also be forbearing and avoid harbouring evil thoughts. Another story by Liezi, "*Haishang Ou Niao*" ("Seagulls on the Sea"), is about a man who lives by the sea and loves seagulls. He would go to the seaside and play with them at the break of dawn every day. Hundreds of gulls would gather near him and not fly away. His father said, "I heard that seagulls have a liking for you. Catch a few for me so that I too can play with them." The next morning, the man went to the seaside as usual, only to see the seagulls hovering in the sky; none of them came down to him. Hence, it is said that one's inner feelings come through although one may try to hide one's thoughts; even birds can intuitively read one's mind.

Here is another story by Liezi, "*Zheng Ren Shi Lu*" ("The Man from Zheng Lost His Deer"), which calls for much critical and logical thinking about one's conscience. The six characters in the passage are a woodsman from Zheng, a passerby, his roommate, the magistrate, King Zheng, and his adviser.

One day by chance, a woodsman from Zheng saw a deer in the open field; he shot and killed it. Fearing that others might have seen it, he quickly covered the deer with banana leaves. He was very much pleased with what he had done. However, he soon forgot where the deer was hidden and thereupon thought that it was only a dream. On his way home, he kept chanting and recalling the whole incident. A passerby who heard him then searched and found the deer and took it home. He told his roommate, "The woodsman dreamt that he had killed the deer but did not know where the deer was hidden. Now that I have found the deer, his dream must be true."

The roommate said, "Did you dream that a woodsman had the deer? Was there really a woodsman? Now that you have the deer, doesn't it mean that the dream of the woodsman must be true?" The passerby said, "Now that I have the deer, what is the point of me knowing whether his dream or my dream is true?" In the meantime, the woodsman arrived home, very much depressed about his lost deer. That night, he had a dream about the hiding place and the passerby who heard his words. The next morning, he followed his dream and located both the passerby and the deer. The woodsman took the passerby to the magistrate, suing for the return of the deer.

The magistrate said, "Initially the woodsman really killed and possessed the deer but thought it was a dream. He then dreamt that he actually killed the deer and it was real. The woodsman discovered that the passerby had really taken his deer, and so he wants to get it back. Furthermore, the roommate also said that the passerby took the deer from another man's dream, assuming that no one owned the deer. Since the deer is here, please divide it equally between the two men."

The case was brought up to King Zheng, who jokingly said, "How wonderful! Can it be that the magistrate will soon dream of dividing the deer?" He then sent the case for a hearing before his chief adviser. The adviser said, "I cannot distinguish between realities and dreams. If realities and dreams have to be differentiated, only Emperor Huang or Confucius was qualified to do so. Now that both of them are dead, who else can do the job? I propose we let the judgement of the magistrate stand."

The moral here is that we must do things with a clear conscience. It was the fear of the woodsman that others would come to know about his deeds, and the dishonest act of the passerby, that led to the case being brought right up to the king. The wisdom of the magistrate might also have caused some eyebrows to be raised. The passerby could have just returned the deer to the woodsman. However, the woodsman was also guilty of killing the deer illegally. Logic dictates that if the woodsman was law abiding in the first place by not killing the deer, the series of unpleasant encounters that followed would not have emerged.

Leave behind a Legacy

Past experience, if not forgotten, is a guide for the future. While flying like a roc and looking beyond your horizon, remember also that what goes up must come down. A time will come when you have to retire gracefully from all work. Make sure you leave behind a legacy for the younger generation. The knowledge in books represents the experiences summed up by our predecessors. It is just like one generation planting the trees under whose shade another generation rests, just as we have reaped the fruit of the labour of our forefathers. When we go through ups and downs in life, we will be able to strike a sympathetic chord with those who already walked the path we tread.

During the time of Jin dynasty in China, about 1,700 years ago, Emperor Hui could hear people shouting at the top of their voices outside his palace. At the time, there was a nationwide famine. The emperor asked his right-hand men what was going on. When told that it was due to famine, the emperor asked, "What is famine?" "Famine means there is no rice to eat," one of them replied. At this point, the emperor asked innocently, "Why don't they eat meat?"

If Emperor Hui had been living among the people, he would have known about their hardships and would not have uttered such ridiculous and childish words. Benjamin Franklin, one of the Founding Fathers of the United States, said, "The things which hurt, instruct." Emperor Hui, who was born with a silver spoon in his mouth and had never experienced hardship in life, would never be able to understand the suffering of the poor.

History repeats itself in a cycle: poverty begets diligence and thrift; diligence and thrift beget riches and honour; riches and honour beget arrogance and dissipation; arrogance and dissipation beget licentiousness and leisure; licentiousness and leisure beget poverty again. As poverty also gives rise to a desire for change, it begets diligence and thrift. This cycle is repeated as generations come and go. However, when you take heed not to repeat that history, then you can inculcate in your next generation the right attitude in living. The causality between cause and effect never fails. You can leave behind a legacy that will benefit your family members specifically and the public generally, all of whom will treasure it. It will be a testimony of you as a person to be respected and admired.

Be Proactive

In Aesop's fable "The Wild Boar and the Fox," the boar stood under a tree, rubbing his tusks against the trunk. A fox passing by asked him the reason for doing so, since there was no imminent danger either from the hunters or hounds. The wild boar replied, "I do it advisedly, for it would never do to have to sharpen my weapons just at the time I ought to be using them." This is called preparing for danger in times of peace. It is similar to this ancient Chinese saying: "Maintain an army for a thousand days to use it for an hour." Thus, you ought to be motivated to have forward planning and be proactive in life.

When you are proactive in your work, it is the consequence of your good and forward planning. You know what is to be done ahead of time, so that you always have a clear picture of the task to be performed. This is vital in ensuring that all potential problems are dealt with proactively, with a contingency plan in place. In this way, you are much more likely to achieve your goals than when you are passive in your attitude.

Make Hay While the Sun Shines

When you view yourself with the right perspective and realise that nobody owes you a living, you will stop murmuring and procrastinating. This will lead to a burning desire to crystallise your thinking and make things happen. *The Fir Tree,* written by Hans Christian Andersen in 1845, shows the importance of appreciating what you already have and enjoying life to the fullest.

The story is about a pretty little fir tree which was not happy with what it was. It wanted to be tall like the pines and firs which grew around it. It did not enjoy the sunshine, the birds, or the rosy clouds. The little fir tree complained all the time. One day, the wood-cutters chopped down the tallest trees and stripped them of their branches, to the consternation of the little fir tree. It knew not the destination of the fallen trees. When the fir tree learnt from a stork that they were travelling on several new ships, it desired to travel by sea (even though it did not know what the sea looked like).

The fir tree ignored the advice of the sunbeam, the wind, and the dew, who all said to enjoy life while it was in its youth. Later, when other trees were cut down and decorated for Christmas, it changed its mind and wanted to be adorned beautifully and brightly. Its dream came true one day, but while trembling for joy, one of the candles fell among the green leaves and burnt some of them. After the holiday, the fir tree was dragged upstairs to be hidden from sight. In its loneliness, the fir tree recalled all the good times which it failed to appreciate and enjoy. It was too late to regret. The fir tree was chopped into small pieces and burned, becoming history. Its life was past.

You now know that the fir tree had never been happy because it was not appreciative of what it was and always compared itself with others. When you are motivated to make hay while the sun shines, you are living a life of fulfillment. Opportunities never come to those who wait, and they come to pass very swiftly, so capture them in the days of your youth. It is said that losers see a thunderstorm while winners see a rainbow. Under the same circumstances, losers ignore the rainbow and think a thunderstorm is imminent when they see a few drops of rain; winners, however, see the living hope in the rainbow and take no notice of the rain. Do you want to be a pessimist or an optimist? Make hay while the sun shines.

Consult the Right Person

A man from Lu wanted to enter a city gate while holding a long pole. Initially, he held the pole vertically, but the pole could not pass through the gate. He then tried to hold it horizontally, but it still could not pass through. He was out of ideas. An old man came along and said, "I am not a saint but I have experiences in everything. Why don't you cut the pole in two at the middle?" The man followed his advice, and after cutting the pole in half, he was able to pass through the gate. (Pei 2007c)

There are many wise men around you. It is your task to find out for yourself who can help with your problems and not to worsen the situation. You must be sharp enough to avoid consulting those who are not competent. You must know how to consult the right people. Avoid trusting people who run with the hare and hunt with the hounds.

Strive for Excellence

In order to truly excel, you have to walk the extra mile in all your undertakings. You will be a man of distinction when others recognise your excellent work. Always get to know the two most important persons in your life; stand high and see far; know the importance of goal settings; and execute a well-designed plan to achieve your goals. Shun the pitfalls of the thirty-six stratagems and be highly motivated so that you can walk tall and fly like a roc in a borderless sky. You will be conscientious in doing your work and leave nothing to chance. You have integrity, self-confidence, and excellence as your hallmarks.

To strive for excellence, you need to have patience and endurance. If you work at it hard enough, sooner or later, you will grind an iron rod into a needle.

Mr Not-Much-of-a-Difference

In 1924, Hu Shi, an internationally renowned author and educator, wrote a classic book about a casual person in China. This satirical masterpiece is an absolute gem. I would like you to share in his humour.

> Do you know who the most famous person in China is? The mere mention of this person will definitely ring a bell in you, because he is known to everyone, everywhere. His surname is *Difference* and his given name is *Not Much of a*. He is the resident of every province, every district, and every village. You must have seen him before and heard others talking about him. Indeed, his full name, Mr Not-much-of-a-difference, is the pet phrase of everybody, for he is representative of all the people in China.
>
> The facial features of Mr Not-much-of-a-difference are not much different from yours and mine. He has a pair of eyes that do not see clearly; has two ears that hear vaguely; has a nose and mouth that are not too particular about smell and taste; and has a brain which cannot be said to be small; his thinking is nowhere near being meticulous.
>
> He always says, "As long as all things are not much of a difference, it should be all right already. Why then be so fussy?"
>
> While still in his childhood, his mother sent him on an errand to buy red sugar, but he came back with white. When he was scolded by his mother, he just

shook his head and uttered, "Red sugar, white sugar, aren't they not much of a difference?" When he was in school, his teacher asked him to give the name of a province. He gave the wrong answer which, though it sounded quite similar to the correct one, was totally off tangent. When the teacher corrected him, he said that there was not much of a difference, because the two provinces sounded almost the same.

Later he became an assistant in a shop dealing with money. He knew how to write and count, except that he was not meticulous. His "ten" (written in Chinese as "十") would be written as "thousand" (in Chinese, "千"), and his "thousand" would be written as "ten." The manager of the shop was angry with him each time he made mistakes, but he would just grin and say, "The word 'thousand' (千) has only one stroke more than the word 'ten' (十); aren't they not much of a difference?"

One day, he had an urgent matter to attend to and had to travel to Shanghai by train. He walked leisurely to the railway station and arrived two minutes late; the train had left without him. He stared at the smoke from the moving train, shook his head, and said, "I'll have to wait till to-morrow to leave. Leaving today and leaving to-morrow is still not much of a difference, but I feel that the company managing the train is a bit too serious. Doesn't leaving at 8.30 and leaving at 8.32 not much of a difference?" He muttered a complaint while walking home because deep in his heart, he still could not understand why the train did not wait two minutes for him.

One day he was seriously ill, so he directed his family members to quickly go and call for Mr Wang on Eastern Street. They hurried out to look for Mr

Wang but could not locate him. Instead, they found another physician named Mr Wang, who was on Western Street, and brought him to the house; this doctor was an expert in treating cows.

Even though Mr Not-much-of-a-difference was bedridden, he knew that the wrong person had been summoned. Since his condition was acute and he was suffering in pain, he couldn't wait for the right physician to come. He thought to himself, *Fortunately, the two Wangs are not much of a difference; I might as well let him try it out on me.* The cow physician then approached Mr Not-much-of-a-difference and treated him the way cows were treated. Within an hour, he kicked the bucket.

Before Mr Not-much-of-a-difference breathed his last, he stammered as he said, "The living . . . and . . . the . . . dead . . . are . . . not . . . not . . . not . . . much . . . of . . . a . . . difference . . . . As . . . all . . . things . . . are . . . not . . . much . . . of . . . a . . . difference . . . why . . . must . . . you . . . be . . . so . . . serious?" After uttering this maxim, he died.

Following his death, everybody praised Mr Not-much-of-a-difference for being able to see through life and straighten out his thinking. Everybody commented that he had never been serious throughout his life. He did not bother to square accounts with anyone. What a person of moral integrity he had been. For this, after his demise, he was given a title: Grand Master of Accommodating. His fame spread far and wide. As time went on, more and more people emulated his example and became like Mr Not-much-of-a-difference. However, henceforth China became known as a nation of lazy people. (Hu Shi 2008)

The moral is that we ought to be serious in all the things that we do. Anything that is worth doing is worth doing well; you should turn your wishful thinking into reality. When you focus on doing one thing at a time, you tend to be meticulous in your planning. It may take up time initially, but it pays off handsomely once you execute your plans zealously. If you want to be an accomplished person in life, especially on the scholastic field, follow these principles: always be examining, be cautious in thinking, be able to discriminate, and put your knowledge into practice. When you examine and question while you are learning, you are absorbing the best of everything and think on your own. When you apply what you have mastered in your daily life, you will achieve your goals. Walk the extra mile in all your endeavours to achieve excellence.

Cheap Tricks Never Last

This proverb is about a donkey in ancient Guizhou, China, which had exhausted its tricks. A tiger was walking around, looking for food to eat. When he came upon the donkey, he was frightened, because he had never seen this strange animal before. He hid himself in the bush to observe the donkey's movements. The tiger slowly drew near to the donkey, but when the donkey began braying at him, he fled. The humiliated tiger later returned to face the donkey once again. This time, the donkey did not bray but began kicking his hooves up. The trick was repeated, and the tiger knew that the strange animal could not do anything more, so it was not a threat to him at all. He attacked the donkey and devoured it.

You should therefore learn that cheap tricks, which never last, are not to be feared. In life, a person without skills is not competitive and poses no threat to his opponents.

True Gold Fears No Fire

A person of integrity can stand severe tests; a scholar has great learning and is intellectually enduring. When it is time to evaluate someone's integrity and ability, the one with virtue and genuine talent will pass the test.

There was a king in ancient China who loved to listen to the music played on the *sheng,* a reed pipe wind instrument. He would assemble three hundred musicians to perform together each time he called for a concert to be performed. Nan Guo, who did not know how to play the *sheng,* pretended to be an expert and joined the group of musicians. During the performance, he would act as if he were as good as the other musicians. His inability to play the *sheng* could not be detected because each performance was a group effort. When the king died, his son took over the reign as king. Like his father, the new king also loved the sound of *sheng.* The only difference was that this time the concert was to be a solo performance. Nan Guo knew that he could no longer deceive the king, so he fled the royal court. The incompetent with no skill and character will soon give himself away.

Doing the Right Thing Is Never a Wrong Choice

If doing the right thing is never a wrong choice, then doing the wrong thing is also never a right choice. Hence, it is important for you to ponder carefully before you decide on specific goals. Once you have planned your SMART goals after careful consideration, you should be on the right track to eventually look beyond your horizon.

Small Steps

Louis Sachar (1954-present), an award-winning author of fiction and educational books for children, typically wrote for only two hours each day; when he was asked why, his answer was simple: "Small steps." "Every time I start a new novel," he said, "it seems like an impossible undertaking. If I tried to do too much too quickly, I would get lost and feel overwhelmed. I have to go slow, and give things a chance to take form and grow." (Louis Sachar 2006)

Sachar's novel, *Small Steps,* is about a young man by the name of Armpit who wanted to turn over a new leaf after being released from Camp Green Lake, a juvenile detention center in Austin, Texas. However, the stigma dogged him and no one gave him a chance. The only person who trusted him was Ginny, his ten-year-old neighbour with cerebral palsy. Slowly but surely, they learnt to take small steps. When everything seemed to be smooth sailing, X-Ray, an acquaintance from Camp Green Lake, disrupted their plan with a get-rich-quick scheme. As fate had it, this led to a chance encounter with teen pop sensation Karia Deleon. This marked the beginning of a new chapter of a whole new life for Armpit. (Random House 1995-2008)

Louis Sachar did well to bring out his views on the nature of celebrity, race, and the intricate networking that determines a person's life. In order not to deviate from your path, you ought to remember that doing the right thing is never a wrong choice, but a small step in the right direction.

Into the Wild

On this note, I recommend reading *Into the Wild,* a book by Jon Krakauer about Christopher McCandless, a twenty-four-year-old adventurer who was world-weary even though he was from a well-to-do family.

Chris hitchhiked to the Alaskan wilderness north of Mount McKinley on 28 April 1992, hoping to conquer the harsh reality of nature with only a ten-pound bag of rice and minimal gear. Chris was idealism personified; he wanted to live off the land for a few months. Four months later, his decomposed body was found by a moose hunter. He had died after eating seeds from wild poisonous potatoes. (Harpo Productions 2008)

This book was made into a movie, and I happened to see it on TV. Was Chris doing the right thing when he rejected materialism for the idealism of his own? Was it right for Chris to leave behind his family members, who must have missed him because he had lost touch with them for years? Had he chosen a goal that was too difficult for anyone to achieve, bearing in mind the limitations of his physical and emotional strengths? Is it right to say that you can admire his determination and courage without emulating his action? Was risking his life the right thing to do? Was it the wrong choice? This should remind you that your goals must be SMART and your decision must be based on common sense.

Dare to Be Different

In the olden days, people from poor families had only two options. Firstly, they could be an apprentice in a shop and spend years sweeping the floor, doing errands, and learning some elementary craftsmanship. Secondly, they could just leave home for greener pastures. Girls were normally married off early, without any opportunity to go further than that. Now, however, you can aspire to be whatever you want to be.

Reading makes a person, and books constitute a means of gaining knowledge. In ancient times, people found it exceedingly difficult to interact and communicate with one another intellectually. Ideas could not be conveyed quickly or expressed effectively in the written form. People wrote on oracle bones, tortoise shells, papyrus cloth, and tree bark. As such, human progress was delayed by this state of affairs.

With the emergence of the printing press, tens of thousands of books could be printed rapidly to help popularise reading.

The institutions of higher learning all over the world are now able to make much headway because of the efficacy in the field of printing. Cheap paperback editions of novels and books are increasingly popular and affordable. Furthermore, the easy availability of on-demand self-publishing services is a welcome initiative to authors who wish to have their books widely circulated.

Time has changed, and you now have the opportunity to read books and surf the Internet for information to make your life better. You should also know that mastering the various functions of a computer will make you more productive than someone who is computer illiterate. Strive to be an expert in what you do. Start early. Have a solid foundation and the passion to excel in your career. When you possess a high degree of technical or professional proficiency in your field of work, you will have the privilege to call the tune and also be highly respected for your knowledge and expertise.

Zhuang Zi wrote a story about a master butcher who had acquired such excellent skills in slaughtering ox that King Huiwang of Liang was greatly impressed. The master butcher showed very fine-motor coordination in his work, and this prompted the king to ask him how he could slaughter an ox with such ease.

The butcher respectfully explained to the king that it was the result of hard work, practice, and perseverance. He recalled that when he first started, he saw before him only individual whole oxen. However, after three years of practice, the butcher said he no longer saw whole oxen but merely their muscles, tendons, and bones. He could then cut the open joints of those parts without touching the bones. The butcher then added that for more complicated joints of tendons and bones, he could concentrate and gently manoeuvre his knife to cut at the right point for the parts to yield like crumbling earth. The king then praised the butcher and commented that he had learnt many valuable lessons from him.

The idiom "Seeing no ox as whole" is now used to describe superb skills and highly efficient work. The butcher received the attention of the king because of his talent and skills manifested while slaughtering an ox. Similarly, you will be singled out as extraordinary in your performance when you learn to equip yourself with skills that can only come by through diligence and learning.

There was a rich man who wanted to build a new mansion as magnificent as his friend's three-storey building. When his contractor started to dig the foundation to be followed by the laying of bricks, the rich man asked what he was doing. When the contractor explained that he was beginning construction, the rich man said, "I only want the third storey built, without the first and second." The contractor was furious and retorted, "How can I put up the third storey without first completing the lower two?" The rich man, being stupid, could not comprehend what the contractor was saying and insisted that only the third storey was to be built. This story of the rich man wanting a castle in the air was recorded in *One Hundred Parables*.

Instead of building castles in the air and daydreaming, you ought to be realistic when you make your plans, visions, and desires become a reality. To excel in life, you have to start on a firm foundation. Learn from your peers, read widely, manage your time wisely, enroll in courses, budget well, and do not become a slave to credit cards. Work smart, play hard, and study diligently to be an authority in your chosen career. When we fail to build a mound for want of the last basket of earth, we fail to attain success for want of a final effort. On the other hand, though only a basket of earth is used to level a piece of land, it still shows that progress is made. Mencius gave us some very profound yet meaningful words of advice when he said that "a well that is dug 90 percent but has yet to produce water is still considered a deserted well." You must therefore carry through your plan until it is fully executed.

In June 1936, Margaret M. Mitchell (1900-1949) wrote the famous book *Gone with the Wind*; she won the Pulitzer Prize in 1937. The novel, the only one she wrote, was made into a classic motion picture in 1939. She wrote:

> If the novel has a theme it is that of survival. What makes some people able to come through catastrophes and others, apparently just as able, strong, and brave, go under? It happens in every upheaval. Some people survive; others don't. What qualities are in those who fight their way through triumphantly that are lacking in those who go under . . . ? I only know that the survivors used to call that quality "gumption." So I wrote about the people who had gumption and the people who didn't. (Mitchell 2000-2008)

"Gumption" means resourcefulness or initiative. A person who works hard but does not seem to have much gumption cannot go far. Thus, when you are diligent and have gumption, you show resourcefulness, initiative, and common sense. You dare to be different in pursuing your dream; it takes a lot of gumption, for example, to start up your own business single-handedly. To be able to think and act in a practical way, you need to start from the basics and acquire that quality called gumption.

If you enjoyed reading when you were a child, you probably read books written by the talented Noel Streatfeild (1895-1986) from England. Her classic novels are like the perfect chocolate: deliciously rich yet not sickly sweet. *The Ballet Shoes* was set in London in the 1930s. It is a timeless story about a family's struggle to fulfill their dreams. Three unrelated orphans,

Pauline, Petrova, and Posy Fossil, were adopted by an eccentric explorer and palaeontologist, Great Uncle Matthew (or "Gum").

The three orphans were brought up as sisters by Sylvia, Gum's selfless great-niece, and her old nurse. One longed to be an actress, another wanted to be an aviator, and the third hoped to become a world-class ballerina. The girls vowed to get their names into the history books, but their ambitions were threatened by financial constraints. Ultimately, Pauline became a talented actress while Posy developed into a great ballerina. Petrova preferred to work in a garage. (Wikipedia 2007) The moral of this book is that you must distinguish yourself by developing a determination with sustained effort to achieve your goals in life.

There were many lectures recorded in *Yan's Family Motto* (*Yanshi Jiaxun*) during the Sui dynasty. One of them was called "PhD Selling Donkey" ("*Boshi Mailu*"). Incidentally, China's history stretches back almost five thousand years, and PhD degrees were granted thousands of years ahead of the universities in the West.

A long time ago, the talent of a PhD holder was tested by a man who wanted to sell his donkey. He requested the PhD holder to write a "For Sale" notice for him. This PhD holder wrote a long passage on three pages of paper, but the word "donkey" did not appear, and there was no indication that the man was selling anything. (Pei 2007b) This story shows that learned people with no common sense are not the best candidate for any job.

Learn the Chinese Language

In order to stretch your horizons and go global, you should learn the Chinese language (if you have not already learnt the language of China's 1.3 billion people). China has become a land of opportunity for international students, artists, researchers, and investors. The five thousand years of Chinese culture is there for you to explore. You should therefore learn the language of the most populous country in the world; China is a happening place.

The ancient civilisation is going to reshape the world. China has already taken steps to encourage Mandarin study through its Confucius Institutes, designed to promote Chinese language and culture worldwide. If you know both English and Mandarin or are multilingual, you command a premium in the economic market.

There Are More Solutions than Problems in Life

You may find the story of Sir Walter Raleigh and Queen Elizabeth I relevant and interesting here. The young Raleigh was among the crowd watching the Queen passing from the palace to her boat. As she approached where Raleigh stood, she glanced at the ground and hesitated for a while. The proactive Raleigh quickly surged forward and placed his cloak over a muddy spot, bowing low with respect before the Queen. The Queen smiled graciously at him before stepping on the cloak and walking to her boat. The Queen later made Raleigh part of her household. (Kelly 2007) The Queen had a problem, and Raleigh had a solution. Indeed, if there is no solution to a problem, then that problem does not constitute a problem in the first place.

Have a Human Touch

As a tall tree catches the wind, you are liable to be attacked when you are in a high position. If you are weak in your interpersonal skills, then take action to improve them. With an improved emotional intelligence, you will have the empathy to understand others. As a leader, you must know your subordinates well enough to assign them jobs commensurate with their abilities. Always remember that you are dealing with human beings with fast-changing emotional feelings. Hence, if you deal with personnel problems in your company, you will have the freedom to be like "the body moving its arm and the arm moving its fingers." Your human touch can turn your potential enemies into your friends. You will then have fewer problems and conflicts in life.

Those who live near the water know the characteristics of fishes, while those who live near the mountains understand the voices of birds. Those who are strong in interpersonal skills have good emotional intelligence and understand people. Therefore, when you have a human touch, you are empathetic in nature. You will be popular among your friends and colleagues. Your understanding of others will also be greatly appreciated by the disadvantaged. The following anecdote by Liezi, *Mei Zhe Zi Mei* ("The Pretty Knows She Is Pretty"), is both interesting and refreshing.

The Pretty Knows She Is Pretty

Mr Yang was on his way to Song when he met a man who had two wives: one was pretty and the other was a plain Jane. However, the man loved the plain wife more than he loved the pretty one. When asked for the reason, he answered, "The pretty one knows she is pretty. I don't. The plain Jane knows she is plain. I don't. A bad person knows he is bad. I don't." Yang said, "I shall remember it. The saint behaves like a saint of his own choice."

The man knew in his heart why he loved the plain wife more than the pretty one. We don't. We just could guess that he might have the human touch in looking at his plain wife. He acted on his own volition. Similarly, you are what you are of your own choice and need not always live on others' opinions. This saying is appropriate: "Old wood best to burn, old wine best to drink, old friends to trust, and old authors to read." You will be wiser as you grow older.

"The Guest"

You may find this short story written by Albert Camus (1913-1960), an Algerian-born French essayist who won the Nobel Prize in 1957, worth reading. This story was about a schoolteacher who took in a prisoner to stay in his school quarters and developed a good friendship with him. However, the teacher was in a dilemma: should he hand the prisoner over to the police? He allowed the prisoner to choose his own path at the crossroads. One way would lead to the desert and the other to the police station. The prisoner preferred captivity to freedom. When the teacher returned to his school house, there was a threatening note on the blackboard: "You handed over our brother. You will pay for this." (eNotes.com 2008)

You may judge for yourself on the human touch shown by both the teacher and the prisoner. There was a freedom of choice for both of them, and it was their conscience which had the final say. How about the feeling of the teacher who had been wrongly accused by the supporters of the prisoner? Did it pay for the teacher to show compassion to the prisoner? Only you can give your own value judgement.

Be Realistic and Steady

In our materialistic society, people tend to curry favour with the rich, the famous, and the powerful. They play up to those in power for their fame, status, and influence. Hence, when you are in power, beware of those who claim to be your true friends. The fact of life is that when you are no longer influential, these so-called friends disappear.

During the Han dynasty, Zhai Gong had power and influence; his house was always full of guests, and there was also plenty of wine for visitors. However, when he fell out of power, there was not even the shadow of a guest to be seen. Later, when he staged a comeback, his courtyard began to be filled with visitors and the incessant stream of horses and carriages returned. Zhai Gong was so driven beyond forbearance that he posted this sign on his door: "Long-standing friendship is seen in times of life and death; attitude is seen in times of poverty and wealth; friendly relation manifests itself in times of honour and dishonour." The sign exposed the hypocrisy of human relationships.

It is said that when a person is old and retired from his work, he must have three old treasures with him: old friends, an old spouse, and old savings. With these three "old faithfuls," his retirement life will not be lonely or pitiable. Therefore, when you are young, invest your time in making good friends, spend quality time with your family members (especially your spouse, who is with you in sickness and in health), and start your financial planning early. When you are kind to others, you life will be much more pleasant, because you will have more friends than enemies.

Be Learned and Practical

In the quest for knowledge, you must make sure that you do not study mechanically. You may be very knowledgeable and highly qualified, but some skills cannot be learned from books alone. You need to have hands-on experience as well. Zhuangzi wrote an interesting story on learning through the conversation between Duke Huan and a wheelwright named Pian.

Duke Huan was reading a book in the upper hall, while Pian was chiseling a wheel in the courtyard below. Pian stopped working on his wheel and climbed the stairs to ask Duke Huan,

"May I be bold enough to enquire what words are in the book Your Grace is reading?"

"The classic of a well-known sage," answered the duke.

"Is the sage still alive?"

"He is already dead."

Wheelwright Pian then said, "In that case, you are reading the dregs left behind by a dead man!"

Duke Huan said, "How dare a wheelwright like you comment on what I read? If you can explain yourself, I will forgive you; otherwise, you will die."

Wheelwright Pian said, "I view it from the perspective of my work. I chisel at a wheel. If I do it too slow, the chisel slips over the surface and does not stay put. If I hurry, the chisel gets stuck and does not cut well. If I am neither too slow nor too fast, then I can control my hands well in accordance with the response of my heart. I can explain this to my son, but he will never be able to inherit this skill from me. That is why at the age of seventy, I am still at work making wheels. The sage who could not pass down his wisdom is already dead. Therefore I say the book you are reading is nothing but the dregs of a dead man."

Do you think that the wheelwright was logical in his reasoning? If not, why? Is reading a book the same as chiseling at a wheel? Is intellectual intelligence the same as physical intelligence? Do you read with understanding? If the wheelwright is right, do you need to read anymore? Hence, other than your academic qualifications, you also have to be critical in your thinking and be quick-witted and practical in your life. Apply what you have learnt in your daily life as far as possible.

In lower primary school, my teacher read us Aesop's story of "Belling the Cat"; the whole class was mesmerised. The mice met to devise a plan for them to escape from their enemy, the cat. If only they could hear the cat coming, then they might have enough time to run away. It was an urgent issue that needed a quick solution so that they would not live in constant fear of the cat's claws. Many plans were proposed but thrown out because they were not feasible. Finally one young bright spark suggested, "I have a simple and yet effective plan. All we need to do is to hang a bell about the cat's neck. When we hear the bell ringing, we will then know that our enemy is coming." The mice were delighted at the plan, only to be told by an old mouse, "I must say that the plan of the young mouse is excellent. However, may I ask: Who will bell the cat?"

You must always remember that it is always easier said than done. Both the theory and the practical aspects of life must be taken into account in solving problems.

Enlarge Your Network

The beauty of networking is its swiftness in providing you with any information you want. It goes beyond the transfer of statistics to the accumulation, creation, and intellectual exchange of knowledge. There is the presence of synergy when you do your networking with your fellow networkers. You can add extra dimensions to new information and create new ideas for your study, career, or business. Networkers can therefore collectively enrich and exchange your knowledge for the benefit of others. You will be highly motivated when you know that through knowledge networking, valuable information comes to you twenty-four hours a day.

Each additional academic degree will be your slight edge, when you know how to apply the extra knowledge gained in your practical life and business. You will not feel like a square peg in a round role at your workplace if you know how to enlarge your network and adapt yourself to changing conditions. Here is another story about business acumen:

A man from the state of Lu was an expert in weaving hemp sandals, while his wife was good at weaving fine white silk. The couple planned to move to the state of Yue. Someone told him, "You will surely be in dire financial straits." "Why?" he asked. "Hemp sandals are for walking but the people of Yue walk barefoot; white silk is meant for making hats but the people of Yue go about without any headgear. If you go to a place where your talent and skills are of no use, how can you avoid being poor?" (Pei 2007a)

Both the husband and wife had no sense of doing business. They lacked this information, which was vital in business planning. When you plan ahead, study the relevant subject, and attend training, you will know what you are doing and avoid the pitfalls faced by the couple.

Your Driving Force

When you have motivation, you have both "motive" and "action." The motive will make you proactive, and motivation will become your driving force. Motivation can therefore be likened to a motor that enables you to fly like a roc. Nothing runs without motivation, for without motive and action, the motor can come to a standstill, stutter, or perish completely. With some encouragement and motivation, you can revive the motor so that it is fit not only for the Grand Prix but to fly to Mars.

The rat race in our competitive world requires you to know that motivation and staff management may just be platitudes, because everyone talks about them. Nevertheless, it is still very important in the workplace and office, where your bosses rack their brains in scheming with motivation, which is an important factor in management. Many academics subscribe to the theory that it is not easy to motivate someone else; you can only create a situation in which they can be motivated. However, it is generally accepted that motivation that has elements of coercion and rewards is temporary. Once you remove these elements, the motivation ceases. The only motivation that is permanent is an attitudinal change; by changing your heart, nothing can extinguish your self-confidence.

If you lack interest in your job, then you should search your inner heart for the causes. Do you lack motivation because of your position? If not, perhaps it is a temporary lapse in interest. You may have to look for greener pastures where you can find joy, satisfaction, and incentive to pursue your dream. Work with motivation because it is the engine of your life. Take note that motivation is a *sine qua non* for a job well done.

Before you decide to change your job, ask yourself what it would be like if you were without a job and without an income. If you were to describe your job, which advantages would you single out to prove it a worthwhile effort to stay on? If you cannot think of one, then you are a square peg in a round hole. Run for your life before your boss runs after yours.

At this juncture, I want to bring to your attention the importance of having real ability and learning. *The Gambler*, a novel written by Fyoder Dostoyevski (1821-1881), a Russian novelist, journalist, and short-story writer, acts as a lesson learnt from the experience of an obsessed gambler.

The Gambler

This novel was written under pressure; Dostoyevski managed to finish it in six weeks. Alexei Ivanovitch vowed to quit gambling the moment he made even at the roulette wheel. He fell in love with a beautiful young woman who did nothing except humiliate him. Toward the end of the novel, Alexei won a fortune at the casino, against all odds. We are not to pass value judgement on Alexei as to his windfall. How could Dostoyevski complete a world-class novel in such a short time? His obsession with gambling had made him a bankrupt, and he was plagued with debts and frequent epileptic seizures. (Amazon 2002) Any normal person under those kind of circumstances would have been totally deranged.

He survived the ordeal because he had such great writing skill. His vast hands-on experience in gambling allowed his trends of thought to go on in a steady stream the moment he started writing. If Dostoyevski had not been in the trade for a long time for his experience to accumulate, he would not have come out with the thrilling story line. This shows that learning is a continuous process; success is the progressive realisation of your dream. You may not know the exact time your dream will come true, but you know that it will, sooner or later.

John Ray (1627-1705) was an English naturalist who published his *Collection of English Proverbs* in 1670. You may know this as a Mother Goose nursery rhyme:

> "If wishes were horses beggars would ride,
> If turnips were watches, I would wear one by my side.
> If 'ifs' and 'ands' were pots and pans
> There would be no work for tinkers' hands!"

If wishes could make things happen, then even destitute people would have everything they wanted. However, when you possess the inherent power of positive thinking in making things happen, you will be what you want to be and feel satisfied. It is vital that you let this invisible force dwell in you. Hence, it is useless to merely wish; you must take action to achieve results. You must have the motivation to be diligent and not be slothful. Bring along your solid food when you have eaten your fill, and have an umbrella with you on a sunny day. That is preparedness.

Ice comes from water but is colder than water; indigo blue is extracted from the indigo plant but is bluer than the plant it comes from, signifying that the pupil has surpassed the master. Confucius said, "Learning without thinking begets ignorance; thinking without learning is dangerous." When you learn and think of the relationship between the ice and water or between the indigo blue and the indigo plant, you will agree that if you stop learning, you will be overtaken by others who are your juniors. There is a Chinese saying with similar teaching: "As in the Changjiang River, the waves behind drive on those before." Each new generation exceeds the last one. A boat sailing against the current will be driven back if it does not forge ahead.

In order to motivate yourself and others, you must first have an understanding of the driving forces behind you, as elaborated in Maslow's behavioural hierarchy, which begins with the basic physiological needs, followed by the needs of security, social recognition, and self-esteem, continuing to the zenith of self-actualisation. At the different stages of your life, you will be motivated to accomplish different tasks that you think are worth doing. Warren Buffett and Bill Gates have now geared themselves towards doing social work to fulfill their dreams of helping the poor and the needy through their extremely generous donations. To them, to give is more blessed than to receive.

The Germans would say it this way: "*Ich fuehle mich Wohl.*" Translated literally, this means "I feel myself well" or "I feel good." The phrase implies that it is vital for you to make yourself feel happy. Your inner joy is your motivational force, and it is all that matters. You should not allow anyone or anything to deprive you of that feeling. You are highly motivated because the voice in you encourages you to be so.

Ivan Sergeyevich Turgenev (1818-1883) was a Russian novelist and playwright. In 1852, he wrote *A Sportsman's Sketches,* also known as *Sketches from a Hunter's Album* or *Notes of a Hunter.* This book was based on Turgenev's experience hunting birds and hares. (Encyclopædia Britannica 2013)

Before he wrote this novel, he had wanted to give up writing. As "the spectators could see the chess game better than the players," Turgenev's friends saw in him the great talent in writing and so encouraged him to continue. He returned to literature and wrote many masterpieces. In this case, Turgenev rekindled his motivation after listening to the advice of his friends and put behind whatever obstacles or negative feelings he harboured. His rethinking motivated him to lasting fame.

Ludwig van Beethoven (1770-1827), one of the world's greatest composers, knew that his impaired hearing was incurable and deteriorating. He did not give up but overcame his handicap with determination and went on to produce great pieces of classical music. Helen Keller crossed the obstacles of being deaf and blind by dedicating her life to the education of the disabled.

If you are blessed with physical health, all the more you should unlock your potential and talent. Just talk to successful people and listen to their stories of hardship, sacrifices, achievements, and tremendous motivation. You can also be the one who is telling the similar story one day when you look beyond your horizon.

Be a Good Listener

I want to stress here the importance of emotional intelligence on good communication skill, because people like to speak more than listen. You will surely notice this at get-together and festive gatherings. Generally, people like to tell others their story but are not patient in listening to others. This reminds me of the first line of the often-quoted speech by Mark Antony in Shakespeare's play *Julius Caesar*: "Friends, Romans, countrymen, lend me your ears." When you are willing to lend your ears and be attentive in a conversation, you impress others of your sincerity in wanting to hear what they have to say. As we have two ears and only one mouth, you are being respectful to others when you do not dominate the conversation in social functions; this is social etiquette.

Enjoy Your Life

People who grow up in happiness may fail to appreciate what happiness really means. When you do not appreciate the happy life you enjoy, you take your blessings for granted. Knowing about music, art, and sports is different from loving them, and loving them is not the same as enjoying them. Appreciate whatever you now have, and strive to improve in all aspects of your life.

In ancient China, there were two personalities whose attitudes towards life are now followed by many people. Qian Lou lived in abject poverty but did not want to eat food offered to him. His wife said he was "not troubled by being poor and lowly, not bothered about acquiring riches and honour." This attitude had a tremendous influence on Tao Yuanming (365-427), who detested his official duties and resigned to return to his village to enjoy the beauty and serenity of a leisurely country life. He understood thoroughly the hypocrisy of those in the official circle. We can say that Tao loathed their thick faces and black hearts; he detested how they exploited the thirty-six stratagems. Ironically, Tao made use of the last stratagem, "Best to go away," and called it a day.

Both Qian Lou and Tao Yuanming had their own utopian ideals to reform society; these ideals might not work, but they were nevertheless very principled people worthy of our emulation. The lessons that you can learn from them are that when you do not resort to base acts to get your riches and honour, you can still live a simple and contented life. Look beyond your horizon and be a high achiever who is rich in integrity and wisdom; remain lowly in heart.

Summary

As a journey of a thousand *li* begins with one step, you need to look beyond your horizon by having a specific goal and a plan to achieve it. You can fly the extra mile when you are confident, have a sustainable effort, and are fearless and upright in your thought, speech, and deeds. When you leave behind a legacy worthy of respect and admiration, you can consider yourself as having been successful in life. The Aesop fable "The Wild Boar and the Fox" tells of the importance of being proactive in all your undertakings. When you are young and when opportunities abound, make hay while the sun shines. To do so, you need to consult the right person; the attitude of Mr Not-much-of-a-difference is not to be emulated.

Cheap tricks never last, and gold fears no fire, so make use of your talent to spearhead the horizon of your vision. Doing the right thing is never a wrong choice but a small and sure step in the right direction. A twenty-four-year-old adventurer went *Into the Wild* only to die from eating poisonous seeds; this raises a few critical questions for you to pass your own value judgement. Those with gumption dare to be different. Knowing the Chinese language enables you to command a higher premium in the economic market, just as you have an advantage in the quest for knowledge when you master the English language. You will have more solutions than problems when you have the human touch to be empathetic, are learned and practical, are realistic and steady, and are a good listener. Life is splendid when you look beyond your horizon and become a high achiever.

References

AAA Native Arts (2002-2008), <http://www.aaanativearts.com/article658.html>, accessed 30 Jan. 2013.

Amazon (2002), <http://www.kirjasto.sci.fi/fdosto.htm>, accessed 11 Feb. 2013.

Amazon.com (2007), <http://www.amazon.ca/oh.Thinks-You-Can-Think/dp/customer-reviews/0394831292>, accessed 28 Jan. 2013.

Amin Index (2008), <http://www.ugandamission.net/aboutug/articles/amin/amin6.html>, accessed 14 Apr. 2013.

Ancient Greek Philosophers (2008), <http://www.goatism.org/greeks.htm>, accessed 10 Feb. 2013.

Answers Corporation (2008), <http://www.answers.com/topic/helen-keller>, accessed 21 Dec. 2012.

AoCM (Association of Confucianism Malaysia) *Kong Xue Lun Wen Ji* (*A Collection of Essays on Confucianism*) (Kuala Lumpur, Malaysia, 2002).

AOL (2008), <http://reference.aol.com/article/_a/declassified-female-spies/20060216162209990001>, accessed 14 Feb. 2013.

Baidu (2008a), <http://zhidao.baidu.com/question/15444983. html?si=4>, accessed 11 Mar. 2013.

Baidu (2008b), <http://zhidao.baidu.com/question/2409019. html?fr=qrI3>, accessed 11 Feb. 2013.

Baidu (2008c), <http://tieba.baidu.com/f?kz=243263219>, accessed 12 Dec. 2012.

Baidu (2008d), <http://zhidao.baidu.com/question/46502572. html>, accessed 12 Jan. 2013.

Baidu (2008e), <http://zhidao.baidu.com/question/4959640. html>, accessed 7 Jan. 2013.

Baidu (2008f), <http://tieba.baidu.com/f?kz=175924648>, accessed 8 Sept. 2012.

Baidu (2013a), <http://zhidao.baidu.com/question/15241278. html, accessed 10 April 2013.

Robin Bal (2006-2007), <http://www.fortunewatch.com/ warren-buffet-the-legend/>, accessed 29 Jan. 2013.

BBC (1999), <http://news.bbc.co.uk/1/hi/world/asia-pacific /415612.stm>, accessed 15 Feb. 2013.

Biographies (2008), <http://www.blupete.com/Literature/ Biographies/History/Gibbon.htm>, accessed 7 Feb. 2013.

Bookyards.com (2005), <http://www.bookyards.com/biography. html?author_id=83&author_name=Tolstoy%2C+Leo>, accessed 15 Feb. 2013.

Bulletin Solutions (2003), <http://www.mentalhealthforum.net/ forum/thread33130.html, accessed 28 Oct.2012.

Dong Boyong and Chen Li, *Zhongguo ren de shenji miaosuan* (*The Wonderful Foresight of Chinese*), *Book Two* (Taipei: Hanxin Wenhua Shiye Private Ltd., 1994).

Li Fu Chen, *Si Shu Dao Guan* (*The Four Books in One*) (Taipei, Taiwan: Zhend Da Printing House, 1967).

Classical Jokes (2008), <http://www.baiyun.net/jokes/Classical_ Jokes.htm>, accessed 5 Jan. 2013.

ClearHarmony Net (2001-2006), <http://clearharmony.net/ articles/200601/30898.html>, accessed 19 Oct. 2012.

ClearHarmony Net (2001-2007), <http://clearharmony.net/articles/200710/41834.html>, accessed 24 Feb. 2013.

Cocoa (2008), <http://www.eurococoa.com/cocoa/story/index.htm>, accessed 24 Jan. 2013.

Paulo Coelho, *The Alchemist* (St. Ives: HarperCollins, Clays Ltd., 2002).

Cover and arrangement (2007), <http://www.yesterdaysclassics.com/previews/kelly_raleigh_preview.pdf>, accessed 2 Nov. 2012.

Encyclopedia Britannica (2008), <http://www.britannica.com/eb/article-9073102/Arnold-Toynbee>, accessed 7 Feb. 2013.

Encyclopædia Britannica (2013), <http://global.britannica.com/EBchecked/topic/561069/A-Sportsmans-Sketches>, accessed 8 Feb. 2013

eNotes.com (2008), <http://www.enotes.com/short-story-criticism/guest-albert-camus>, accessed 30 July 2012.

Google (2008a), <http://makoysliterarywritings.blogspot.com/2008/02/be-like-pencil.html>, accessed 25 Aug. 2012.

Google (2008b), <http://www.davincifocus.com/davinci-sleeping-habit.html>, accessed 27 Sept. 2012.

Harpo Productions (2008), <http://www.oprah.com/tows/pastshows/200709/tows_past_20070920_b.jhtml>, accessed 23 Dec. 2012.

Nee Yong Ho, *East Meets West in Education* (Pearson Malaysia, 2009).

Huaxia (2000), <http://www.huaxia.com/wh/jdgs/cydg/00096707.html>, accessed 12 June 2012.

Inspiration Peak (2007a), <http://www.inspirationpeak.com/agi-bin/stories.cgi?record=118>, accessed 3 Feb. 2013.

Inspiration Peak (2007b), <http://www.inspirationpeak.com/shortstories/livingproof.html>, accessed 14 Feb. 2013.

Japan-101.com (2003-2005), <http://www.japan-101.com/government/alberto_kenya_fujimori.htm>, accessed 15 Aug. 2012.

Jiangxi (2006) Lianzhengwang, <http://www.jxlz.gov.cn/system/2006/10/31/002883367.shtml, assessed 22 October 2012

Kelly, M. D. (2007), "The Story of Sir Walter Raleigh," http://www.yesterdaysclassics.com/previews/kelly_raleigh_preview.pdf, accessed on 2 November 2012.

Lee Kuan Yew, *From Third World to First: The Singapore Story: 1965-2000* (Times Media Private Limited, Singapore Press Holdings, Times Editions, 2000).

Le Monde Diplomatique (2008), <http://mondediplo.com/2007/03/08darfur>, accessed 16 Oct. 2012.

Henic Lund (2007), <http://www.bellum.nu/literature/36stratagems.html>, accessed 12 Dec. 2012.

Fu Min, *Zou Chu Jia Shu* (*Walk Out: Letters from Home: A Conversation with Fou Ts'ong*) (China: Tian Jin Social Sciences Faculty Publishing House, 2005).

M. Mitchell (2000-2008), <http://www.gwtw.org/margaretmitchell.html>, accessed 22 Jan. 2013.

Moment Magazine (2007-2008), <http://www.momentmag.com/Exclusive/2006/2006-08/200608-BrianEpstein.html>, accessed 25 Jan. 2013.

Tan Chin Nam, *Never Say I Assume,* (Selangor, Malaysia: MPH Group Publishing, 2006).

NPR (2008), <http://www.npr.org/templates/Story/Story.php?storyId=4754996>, accessed 24 Jan. 2013.

Ming Loong Pei (2007a), <http://www.chinapage.com/story/business1.html>, accessed 22 Mar. 2013.

Ming Loong Pei (2007b), <http://www.chinapage.com/story/donkey1.html>, accessed 22 and 24 Mar. 2013.

Ming Loong Pei (2007c), <http://www.chinapage.com/story/longpole1.html>, accessed 5 Apr. 2013.

PoemHunter.com (2007), <http://poemhunter.com/poem/home-sweet-home/>, accessed 19 Nov. 2012.

Power Sleep (2008), <http://www.powersleep.org/nap.htm>, accessed 25 Oct. 2012.

Random House (1995-2008), <http://www.randomhouse.com/catalog/display.pperl/9780307282231.html>, accessed 18 Mar. 2013.

Louis Sachar (2006), <http://www.kidsreads.com/authors/ausachar-louis.asp>, accessed 16 Jan. 2013.

SciCentral (2005-2008), <http://www.rwanda-genocide.org/index.html>, accessed 16 Dec. 2012.

Liu Si (2005), Hou Hei Xue (The Study of Thick Face and Black Heart) (Beijing: Economic Daily Publisher).

Hu Shi (2008), <http://www.skhsbs.edu.hk/chi/ref/Artical/166.htm>, accessed 5 Feb. 2013.

Sina.com (2008), <http://iask.sina.com.cn/b/8746181.html?from=related>, accessed 11 Nov. 2012.

Tangyulin (2008), <http://www.wuweixiaozi.com/files1/yulin zhezhi/3/tang_yu_lin/zk.htm>, accessed 24 Mar. 2013.

Tortus Technologies (2002-2004), <http://www.catinthehat.org/history.htm>, accessed 28 Jan. 2013.

TravelChinaGuide (1998-2008), <http://community.travelchina guide.com/forum2.asp?i=42463>, accessed 9 July 2012.

TruthOrFiction.com (1998-2008), <http://www.truthorfiction.com/rumors/c/churchill.htm>, accessed 6 Aug. 2012.

Qiye Wangjing (2008), <http://www.cn21.com.cn/onlinebook/sz36/020727.htm>, accessed 17 Jan. 2013.

Wikipedia (2007), <http://en.wikipedia.org/wiki/Noel_Streatfeild>, accessed 9 Jan. 2013.

Wikipedia (2008a), <http://en.wikipedia.org/wiki/Arthur_C._Clarke>, accessed 8 Oct. 2012.

Wikipedia (2008b), <http://en.wikipedia.org/wiki/Christine_Keeler>, accessed 5 Feb. 2013.

Wikipedia (2008c), <http://en.wikipedia.org/wiki/Douglas_Bader>, accessed 29 Jan. 2013.

Wikipedia (2008d), <http://en.wikipedia.org/wiki/Hippie# Origins_of_a_movement>, accessed 12 Jan. 2013.

Wikipedia (2008e), <http://en.wikipedia.org/wiki/Letter_to_ Chesterfield>, accessed 27 Feb. 2013.

Wordpress.com (2008), <http://ewordpress.wordpress.com/2007/ 10/21/06-the-story-of-pencil/>, accessed 25 Nov. 2012.

Wuweixiaozi (2008), <http://www.wuweixiaozi.com/files1/yulin zhezhi/1/han_fei/5b.htm>, accessed 15 Sept. 2012.

Wang Guang Zhao and Lu Rong, *Zhongguo ren de shenji miaosuan* (*The Wonderful Foresight of Chinese*), *Book Three*, (Taipei: Hanxin Wenhua Shiye, 1994).